Whats4teal

Favourite recipes from the Pigeon Cottage Kitchen.

JANET DAVIES

Copyright © 2017 Janet Davies

All rights reserved.

ISBN: 9781520742847

FOR NINA

"In order to know whether a human being is young or old, offer it food of different kinds at short intervals. If young, it will eat anything at any hour of the day or night".

Oliver Wendell Holmes Senior
(American poet and author)

CONTENTS

INTRODUCTION ... 12

CHAPTER ONE: BREAKFAST ... 15
The 'Full English' – Pigeon Cottage Style ... 15
Builders' Sausage Sandwich ... 16
Ham, Tomato & New Potato Hash ... 17
Perfect 'Dippy' Eggs ... 18
Scrummy Scrambled Eggs ... 19
Poached Eggs ... 20
Omelettes ... 20
French Toast ... 21
John French's Sausage Bread and Butter Pudding ... 22
Frittata ... 23
Nina's Favourite Banana Porridge ... 24
Breakfast Banana Brûlée ... 25
Home Made Yogurt ... 26
Golden Granola ... 27
'Super food' Commuter Muesli ... 28
Smoothies ... 29

CHAPTER TWO: SOUP ... 31
Using Stock ... 31
Soup Essentials - Soffrito or Mirepoix ... 32
Leek and Potato Soup ... 32
Chicken Soup ... 32
Roasted Vegetable Soup ... 33
Roasted Tomato Soup ... 33
Yellow Split Pea Soup with Smoked Sausage ... 34
Lentil & Ham Soup ... 34
Fresh Green Pea & Ham Soup ... 34
Fresh Pea & Roasted Garlic Soup ... 35
Celeriac Soup ... 35
Onion Soup with Cheese Topped Croutons ... 36
Smoked Haddock Chowder ... 36
College Soup ... 37

CHAPTER THREE: MEAT MAIN COURSES 40

Mel's Diner Chilli Con Carne 41
Pigeon Cottage Pie 43
Pigeon Cottage Meat Loaf 45
Magnificent Meatballs 46
Simply Sausages 48
'Sausage Daisy' 48
Cocktail Party Sausages 49
Toad in the Hole 49
Braised Sausages with Beans 51
Suffolk Cider Sausages 52
Puy Lentil & Smoked Sausage Supper 53
Sausage Meat and Bacon Wraps 54
Stews & Casseroles 55
Beef & Beer Stew with Fluffy Dumplings 56
Beef Bourguignon 57
Gorgeous Goulash 59
Rich Oxtail or Ox Cheek Stew 60
Suffolk Cider & Pork Loin Casserole 62
Country Chicken Stew 63
Burgundy Chicken 64
Slow Baked Lamb with Beans 65
Suffolk Lamb Hotpot 67
Perfect English Sunday Roasts 68
Yorkshire Pudding 72
My Sage & Onion Stuffing Mixes 75
Perfect Steak 76
Chubby Chops 77
Pork Chops 77
Lamb Chops 77
Chicken Marinato 78
Boiled or Baked Ham 78
Pot Roasted Beef 80
'Empty Nesters' Liver Recipes 81
Calf's Liver 82
Lamb's Liver with Garlic 82
'The Famous Pork' 83
Thai Prawn Curry 85
Beef in Black Bean Sauce 86

Aromatic Meat Curry 87

CHAPTER FOUR: RICE, GRAINS & PULSES 89

Perfect Basmati Rice 89
Couscous and Bulgur Wheat 90
Kasha 91
Pepper Salad 91
Tabbouleh 91
Risottos 91
Pea & Ham Risotto 91
Pancetta and Rosemary Risotto 92
Mushroom Risotto 93
Pea & Prawn Risotto 93
Puy Lentils with Wine, Rosemary & Sage 93
Puy Lentils with Spinach 94

CHAPTER FIVE: VEGETABLES 96

Mediterranean Roasted Vegetables 98
Winter Roasted Vegetables 98
Vegetable Mash and Purées 98
Cauliflower Cheese 99
Braised Red Cabbage 99
Potatoes 100
Irresistible Roasties 101
Mmmm, My Famous Creamy Mash 101
New Potatoes 102
Brilliant Baked Potatoes 103
Gratins 103
Stock Bake or Boulanger Potatoes 104
Hassleback Potatoes 104
Potato Wedges 104

CHAPTER SIX: SAUCES, DRESSINGS & SEASONINGS 106

Chinese Sauce/Gravy 106
Roasted Onion Gravy 106
Horseradish Sauce 107
Apple Sauce 107
Mint Sauce 107
Bread Sauce 108

Mustard & Parsley Sauce 108
Essential Tomato Sauce 109
Tubby Custard Sauce 109
White Sauces 110
Parsley Sauce 110
Cheese Sauce 110
Béchamel 110
Fresh Mayonnaise 111
Tartare Sauce 111
Aioli 112
Blender Hollandaise 112
Béarnaise Sauce 113
Beurre Blanc 113
Essential Salad Dressing 113
Vinaigrette Salad Dressing 114
Persillade 114
Thai Green Curry Paste 114
Aromatic Curry Powder 115
Garam Masala 115

CHAPTER SEVEN: PASTA 116

Fresh Egg Pasta Dough 116
Lasagne 117
Favourite Pasta Sauces 118
Anna's Bolognese Sauce 118
Essential Tomato Sauce or 'Sugo' 119
Sugo with Chorizo 120
Sugo Puttanesca 120
Sugo Siciliana 120
Sugo Gambero 120
Creamy Mushroom Sauce 120
Spicy Sausage & Mustard 121
Pesto Sauce 122
Carbonara 122
Pasta, Ham & Peas 124
Mac n'Cheese 125

CHAPTER EIGHT: SEAFOOD 128

Spicy Prawns with Courgettes 128
Cod with Spicy Tomato Sauce 129
Baked Salmon or White Fish 130
Pancetta Wrapped Cod 131

Asian Tuna 131
Lowestoft Fish Pie 132
Moules Marinière à la Crème 133
Sharon's Southwold Smoked Salmon Pâté 135
Smoked Mackerel Pâté 135
Melba Toast 135

CHAPTER NINE: SALADS 136

Salade Niçoise 136
Celeriac Remoulade 136
Summer Coleslaw 137
Winter Coleslaw 137
Tomato Salads 138
Greek Salad 139
Tzatziki/Cacik/Raita 140
French Red Rice Salad 140
Cucumber, Olive & Walnut Salad 141
Carrot Salad 142
Bean Salad with Lemon & Mustard Dressing 142
White Bean & Tuna Summer Salad 143
Potato Salad 144
Grandma Foster's Rice & Prawn Salad 144

CHAPTER TEN CAKES & PUDDINGS 146

Classic Sponge Cake 146
Classic Chocolate Cake 147
Chocolate Conserve Cakes 147
Soured Cream & Fruit Conserve Crumble Cake 148
Banana Cake 149
Madeira Cake 150
Lemon & Poppy Seed Cake 151
Very Sticky Ginger Cake 151
Keiller's Dundee Cake 152
English Rice Pudding 153
Indian Rice Pudding 154
Panna Cotta 155
Crumble 156
Fruit Pies 156
Sponge Puddings 157
Tubby Custard Sauce 158
Banana Tubby Custard 158
Chocolate Mousse 158

Mary's Lemon Mousse Pudding 159
Baked Fruit Compotes 161
Rhubarb 161
Gooseberries 162
Plums, Nectarines and Apricots 162
Baked Bananas 162
Baked Apples 162

CHAPTER TWELVE: LEFTOVERS & BUDGET SNACKS 164

Fish Cakes 164
Bubble and Squeak 164
Croquettes 164
New Potato Coins 164
Tortilla 165
Potato Salad 165
Bread leftovers 165
Breadcrumbs 165
Luxury Cheese on Toast 166
Brushetta 166
Croutons 166
Bread Pizza 166
Fridge & Fruit Bowl Orphans 166

KITCHEN EQUIPMENT 175

CONVERSION TABLES 177

ACKNOWLEDGEMENTS i

ABOUT THE AUTHOR ii

WHAT'S4TEAMUM?

INTRODUCTION

For a lot of people the definition of a recipe sounds a little bit like this one.

"Recipe: A series of step-by-step instructions for preparing ingredients you forgot to buy, with utensils you don't own, to make a dish the dog wouldn't eat".

Hopefully, this isn't how anyone will describe the recipes in this book! Pigeon Cottage Kitchen recipes use everyday kitchen equipment, are easy on the washing up, are made from ingredients that can be easily bought in any supermarket or farmers market *and* work every time. They are the result of many years of trial, error and experimentation and, above all, they are delicious, comforting and loved.

My cookery heritage
My mother wasn't taught to cook until she was married in the 1950's. Her mother-in-law showed her how to make classic English family dishes but the only recipe book I ever remember seeing at home was a battered old Be-Ro flour booklet in the pantry. All my mother's recipes were in her head and she made virtually the same ones on the same days week in, week out. We knew that every Wednesday it would be stew with dumplings for supper, on Thursdays it would be boiled gammon with parsley sauce and so on.

I wasn't really taught how to cook at home although, in a family of seven, everyone has a job to help the household run smoothly. So, as well as making my own bed, washing up and running any number of errands, I also learnt how to peel, chop and prepare the very best fruit and vegetables that were grown by my father and his brothers who farmed in Lincolnshire. They sold crops wholesale and they also ran a stall at the local farmer's market; I helped out there too every Saturday and I worked on the farm in the school holidays. I guess that I knew a little bit more about fresh produce than the average teenager even then.

Although I grew up at home with very traditional English fare, as a language student, I was lucky enough to travel to different countries and live with families in France, Germany, Greece and North America. I experienced not only what they ate and how they shopped everyday, but also how they cooked when entertaining or celebrating with friends and family. I had magnificent food cooked from tiny little Parisian kitchens (I so loved the Rachel Koo TV series of the same name) and saw how French women would select a humble potato at the market as carefully as they would a peach. In Greece, we would regularly go snorkelling to catch squid, smash them on the rocks to tenderise them and then cook them over a campfire on the beach. In Canada, I ate my very first 'junk food' but the versions of home made burgers and cream pies I enjoyed there were anything but junk; I had never eaten steak in 1970's England as tender and full of flavour as I did there.

As a student living in Yorkshire, I had to cater for myself. I discovered how to cook up a storm in badly equipped kitchens and with almost no money. I'd never eaten a curry before and in the West Riding there were cheap, family run Asian restaurants everywhere. I came not only to love their hot and spicy dishes, but also learnt how to make truly authentic family recipes, courtesy of the mother of one of my Asian housemates.

When we bought our first house in Norwich, it was absolute heaven to have my very own kitchen to play in. By this time, I had graduated from my battered edition of the 'St Michael All Colour Cookery Book' to the now iconic 'Complete Cookery Course' by Delia Smith. I'd also traded in my battered student cookware for a decent set of Scandinavian saucepans. I still have them and use them almost daily. It wasn't just me who had the cookery bug, most of my friends became very good cooks in the 90's too. Once we had young children, we couldn't afford to go to restaurants or find babysitters every weekend so we'd 'eat out at home' instead.

These days, I have eaten in any number of posh or primitive restaurants the world over and the Pigeon Cottage Kitchen has a bookcase that groans under the weight of lavishly illustrated tomes by the likes of Rick Stein, Keith Floyd, Jamie Oliver, Nigella Lawson, Hugh Fearnly-Whittingstall, Madhur Jaffrey, Sam Clark, Nigel Slater and Claudia Roden. I love reading them, pouring over the illustrations and discovering the stories behind them. I watch every food based TV show going, listen to podcasts of the Food Programme on my daily commute to work and enjoy ferreting out a new market or deli. Most of all, I love nothing better than getting my friends and family around the table to enjoy delicious food and wine, raucous laughter and conversation.

"Whats4teaMum?"

My daughter Nina has always loved to eat well. Her first question as soon as she finished school, mostly delivered by text, would be "Whats4teaMum?" Naturally, once answered, the very next question would be "When will that be ready?" Any mother knows that a hungry teenager's mood and ability to do the obligatory homework improves immeasurably once fed, so you'll find my recipe timings pretty accurate as result! When she was a student in London, I started writing down our favourite family recipes for her and some basics; the type of thing 'cheffy' cookery books don't include such as how to cook a proper 'Full English'. I wrote them one by one, just the way *we* like them. I didn't write them in any particular order, it was usually as the result of a random phone call or text that would start "Mum, how do u make……..?" Eventually, the collection became this book and meant that she could cook up a little bit of home whenever she liked.

So, this recipe book contains my collection of tried and trusted, regular family favourites and I hope some of them will become yours too. These are the dishes that Nina would hope would be on the menu when she'd text me with that all-important daily message. Now, I'm happy to say, she cooks for me when I visit her in London and she's developing her very own repertoire of 'new classics'. All my new recipes are featured on my cookery blog pigeoncottage.com – just add your email address to the 'follow' section and you'll get all my new recipes as soon as they are published. You can also follow me on twitter @pigeoncottage and the Facebook page *Pigeon Cottage Kitchen*.

CHAPTER ONE: BREAKFAST

"I often take exercise. Why only yesterday I had my breakfast in bed."
Oscar Wilde
(Anglo-Irish playwright, novelist, poet)

The 'Full English' – Pigeon Cottage Style

Nothing much beats this treat of a breakfast on a Sunday morning. 'Full English', Sunday papers and a country lane walk to work up an appetite (or walk off the calories) - bliss! The challenge is to cook each individual element perfectly, yet get it all to the table at the same time without anything going cold. It's a simple meal but it takes practice to get it exactly right and work with the constraints of your own kitchen. Nevertheless, my first top tip is to be sure to put your serving plates on to warm *before* you start cooking and have the table laid ready. When I'm making this for a lot of people, I oven cook the sausages first because they take the longest and then add the dishes of mushrooms and tomatoes. I cook everything else on the hob, otherwise there's usually just not enough room for all the pans, and it's much less stressful to manage. Warm a large serving dish on the bottom shelf of the oven and add the sausages, bacon and black pudding as they're ready to keep them warm and then concentrate on cooking the eggs last. In the summer, we cook most of this on the BBQ. Here goes…

Sausages. Only use good quality pork sausages from a reputable butcher. Either cook them for about 40 minutes on the hob in a frying pan on a medium heat so they are brown but still juicy or, oven roast them for 40 minutes at 180°C in a metal tray with a touch of oil (so they don't catch on the bottom of the tray) and a few turns of ground black pepper. Once they are brown and sticky, they're cooked. Never, ever prick them as it just dries them out. Allow at least 2 per person.

Field mushrooms. Allow one large one person or at least 4 to 6 button mushrooms each. Bake them whole in an ovenproof dish (with a lid or cover with foil) on the bottom shelf of the oven for about 20 minutes just dabbed with a little butter and black pepper. Alternatively, slice and lightly sauté them in a non-stick frying pan.

Tomatoes. Allow one fresh one per person or 4 or 5 cherry tomatoes per serving. Halve them, lightly season with a drizzle of olive oil, a drop of sherry vinegar, sea salt and black pepper and grill for 5 minutes. Alternatively, place them whole in a baking dish, stalk side down, with the top lightly scored and anointed with a drop of oil and some seasoning. Oven bake them on the bottom shelf for 8 to 10 minutes.

Bacon. Buy smoked, thickly sliced (collar preferably) bacon and allow at least 2 to 3 pieces per person. Grill it at a high temperature for about 5 minutes until the rind fat is crisp or fry in a pan on the hob. Drain on some kitchen paper to get rid of the excess fat before serving. If your bacon weeps lots of white liquid when it's cooked, that's because it isn't particularly good quality and has been injected with salty water to bulk up the weight – find a reputable butcher to buy it from for best results.

Black pudding. Buy it in a block and cut it into thick coins. Allow one coin per person. Fry it in sunflower or light olive oil for about 5 minutes until crisp on both sides.

Eggs. Try to buy them as fresh as you can – free range for preference. Cook at least one per person. Use a heavy bottomed non-stick pan with a touch of sunflower or light olive oil and fry them for about 4 minutes until the bottom of the white is caramel coloured and lacy and the yolk is still runny. A big bowl of buttery scrambled egg works well too if you're cooking this for a lot of people and want to get everyone to the table at the same time.

Bread. I don't usually serve fried bread as well as this is usually quite enough fat for one meal. I usually serve **toast** instead made from a cut loaf. If you do want fried bread, cook it in the leftover bacon fat.

Freshly made tea is a must. Twinings or Betty's Tearoom blend is our favourite (buy from Betty's direct or online at bettys.co.uk).

Builders' Sausage Sandwich
This is a brilliant Sunday breakfast or snack for about four people. It keeps well for a picnic if you wrap it well in baking parchment and then a layer of

foil and eat it relatively quickly afterwards.

Serves 4
Pre-heat the oven to 180° C
Equipment: Non-stick frying pan, shallow baking dish
Takes: 45 minutes

Ingredients
6 good quality butchers' sausages
2 onions, finely sliced
1 tablespoon of sunflower oil
1 long, large flat bloomer, ciabatta or rustic-style loaf
French mustard
Freshly ground black pepper

Place the sausages in the baking dish with just a little oil and some freshly ground back pepper. Bake in the oven until brown and juicy for about 40 minutes.
Gently fry the sliced onions with the rest of the sunflower oil in the frying pan until browned and crispy.
Slit the loaf open lengthwise; spread a layer of mustard on each side.
Cut the sausages in half lengthwise and layer them evenly on the bottom of the loaf.
Top with the onions, place the second bread layer on top, press down and cut into four thick chunks.
Serve fresh and hot. To eat later, keep it wrapped well in foil.

Ham, Tomato & New Potato Hash

This is a really satisfying and tasty meal for Sunday brunch or a weekday lunch or supper. It's really quick to make if you have leftover cooked ham and cold new potatoes.

Serves 3 - 4
Cooks on the hob
Equipment: Large, wide non-stick frying pan
Takes: 10 minutes to prepare and 20 minutes to cook

Ingredients
60g unsalted butter
1 small onion chopped

Sea salt and freshly ground pepper
130g good quality thick-sliced ham, torn into bite-sized pieces
700g new potatoes, scrubbed and cooked until just tender, then sliced thickly
Freshly grated nutmeg
Cayenne pepper
2 tablespoon of chopped parsley
3 tomatoes, deseeded and roughly chopped
2 tablespoon of double cream
60g grated Cheddar

Melt half the butter in the frying pan over a medium heat. Add the onion, a little sea salt and sauté until the onion is tender.
Add the remaining butter and, when melted, tip in the ham and potatoes and season with lots of black pepper, a good grating of nutmeg, a pinch or two of cayenne and the parsley.
Stir and then press the mixture down into the pan smoothly with a spatula. Leave to cook over a moderate heat, without disturbing it, for 8-10 minutes until browned underneath.
Stir the mixture, scraping up the crusty brown bits from the bottom of the pan. Brown the other side if you have time.
Next, stir in the tomatoes. Press down again, spoon over the cream and scatter over the cheese.
Cover, leave for a couple minutes until the cheese melts, then serve.

Perfect 'Dippy' Eggs

For egg boiling, I always keep a special small saucepan just for that purpose (one that will fit six eggs comfortably) as it will spoil a good pan by coating the inside with mineral deposits from the shells otherwise.
Use the freshest eggs you can, preferably free range or organic because they just taste so much better. There is no difference in flavour between white or brown eggs by the way. This recipe works for large eggs, after all, why would you use any other size to dip your soldiers in?
It's best if the eggs don't come straight out of the fridge (just don't even store eggs in the fridge) as they are more likely to crack and the cooking time will vary. This should produce a properly set white and a runny yolk.
Fresh eggs for soft-boiled eggs are best. Older eggs are better for hard-boiling, as they are easier to peel.
Fill your pan about half full of water, bring it to a rolling boil, gently lower

your egg(s) into the water and cook for four and a half minutes.
Serve immediately with toasted or fresh white bread soldiers.
For a hard-boiled egg with a semi-set yolk to use in a salad or starter, boil for 7 minutes in total. For a completely hard-boiled egg, boil for 9 minutes in total.

*An egg is fresh if it sits horizontally when placed in a glass of water, semi-horizontally means up to a week old, one that floats vertically is stale.

Scrummy Scrambled Eggs

A brilliant breakfast, brunch or supper dish, a plate of hot, buttery scrambled egg on toast is the ultimate fast food. The special ingredient here, a trick I picked up from my friend Kate, is a pinch of English mustard powder. It really makes a difference and adds depth to the flavour. Use fresh, free-range eggs for best results.

Serves 2
Use at least 2 large eggs per person
Equipment: non stick pan
Takes: 5 minutes

Ingredients
4 large eggs
Large knob of unsalted butter
Sea salt and freshly ground pepper
A pinch of English mustard powder

Variations: *chopped chives, grated cheese such as parmesan or crumbled feta, cubes of ham, crisp bacon or pancetta, flaked smoked fish such as salmon or haddock.*

Beat the eggs, sea salt and mustard powder together in a bowl.
Put the pan on a gentle heat, add the butter and wait until it begins to foam gently.
Pour in the egg mixture into the pan and keep stirring until the eggs have thickened.
Serve on a warmed plate with hot buttered toast, plain rye bread or muffins.
Sprinkle with any of your options – chives, crispy bacon, smoked fish,

freshly ground black pepper.
Eat immediately.

Poached Eggs

If you're on a diet, poached eggs offer a less fat laden and tasty alternative to fried or scrambled eggs. A large egg contains about 80 calories and is full of nutrition. Serve with toast or muffins or, my favourite, with fishcakes or potato hash or bubble and squeak. Trendy cafés will serve it with avocados and crispy bacon these days. Only use very fresh eggs or the white will simply disintegrate in the cooking water.

Serves 2
Use 2 large eggs per person at least.
Equipment: small frying pan, kitchen towel
Time: 5 minutes

Ingredients

2 large eggs per person
Water
A tiny drop of white wine or cider vinegar
Sea salt
Options: for Eggs Benedict - 1 tablespoon of wilted spinach, a slice of ham or bacon and a tablespoon of cheese or Hollandaise sauce.
To serve: Hot buttered toast or muffins.

Bring the water to the boil, add a tiny drop of vinegar to keep the white together, crack the eggs into a cup first, stir the water with a spoon to create a little whirlpool and then tip them carefully into the water and leave for exactly a minute. Take the pan off the heat, set aside and leave for 5 minutes or so until the eggs are set. Lift the eggs out gently with a slotted spoon; let the water drain off and season to taste.

Omelettes

I love a golden, buttery omelette – they're quick to make, tasty and great for using up fridge leftovers such as mushrooms, cheese and ham. Add a side salad of green leaves or tomatoes to make a healthy and delicious lunch or supper.

Serves 1, use 3 eggs per person
Equipment: small non-stick omelette pan
Takes: 5 minutes

Ingredients
3 eggs
A knob of butter
A pinch of sea salt
A pinch of English mustard powder
Optional extras: *chopped ham, chopped herbs, grated cheese, thin slices of Brie, sautéed mushrooms, crumbled feta, crispy bacon.*

Heat a small knob of butter with a touch of oil (to prevent burning) in the pan on a medium heat.
Meanwhile, very lightly combine the eggs, a pinch of sea salt and a pinch of English mustard powder in a bowl with a fork.
Once the hot butter is foaming, turn up the hob to its highest setting and then pour the egg mixture into the pan.
Keep the mixture moving on the bottom of the pan by tilting it to and fro. Leave it on the heat to allow it to set slightly on a count of five.
Sprinkle any additional ingredients on top and then tipping the pan slightly, fold the omlette over. It should be golden on the outside and soft on the inside.
Serve and eat straightaway.

French Toast
This is English-style French toast (if that makes any sense at all) not the American kind that is often served with bacon and maple syrup. Children love this breakfast and it always reminds me of the breakfast scene in 'Kramer vs. Kramer' where Dustin Hoffman's character and his son make it together as part of their daily bonding ritual.

Finishing with cinnamon or vanilla sugar makes it extra special. To make your own, just fill a Kilner or screw top jar with golden caster sugar and add in either a stick of cinnamon or a fresh vanilla pod to infuse it. For a more intense flavor, add ground cinnamon to suit your tastes or whizz your sugar up with a vanilla pod in a food processor until it forms fine black specks in the sugar. Make a decent sized batch as it keeps for months.

Serves: 4, although it depends how much you want to eat – I usually allow one large egg and two good thick slices of white bread from a cut loaf per person.
Equipment: a wide non-stick frying pan and a shallow, rectangular dish (a lasagne dish is perfect) for mixing and dunking the bread in the egg mixture.
Takes: 10 minutes

Ingredients
A white cut loaf cut into 8 thick slices - slightly stale bread works best, I prefer mine with the crusts cut off.
4 eggs
150ml milk
Butter
Cinnamon or vanilla sugar
Freshly squeezed orange juice – serve fresh quarters of orange on each plate

Beat the eggs and milk together in the shallow dish.
Melt the butter in a frying pan on a medium heat.
Dip each side of the bread in the egg and milk mixture and then fry them in the butter until golden on each side. Cook as many pieces at one time as the pan will comfortably hold.
Serve hot with freshly squeezed orange juice and a sprinkling of cinnamon or vanilla sugar.

John French's Sausage Bread and Butter Pudding
This is delicious as a weekend brunch dish. We first ate it in Cardiff at our American friends John and Craig's house and we liked it so much that John sent us the recipe. Serve with a green salad or a tomato salad.

Serves 4
Equipment: Large ovenproof soufflé type dish, mixing bowl
Takes: 30 minutes prep, overnight refrigeration, 15 minutes to cook

Ingredients

8 slices of good quality white bread
14 cocktail size cooked sausages or chipolatas cut in half
200g grated strong Cheddar cheese
6 eggs, beaten
250 ml milk
½ teaspoon of salt
½ teaspoon of English mustard powder

Grease a 12cm x 7cm ovenproof casserole or baking dish. Trim the crusts from the bread, cut into cubes and lay them on the bottom of the baking dish.
Cover with the sausages and half of the grated cheese.
In a bowl, beat the eggs, milk, salt and mustard together and then pour the mixture over the bread, sausage and cheese mixture.
Sprinkle the additional cheese over the top.
Cover with foil and refrigerate overnight (essential step).
The following day, take it out of the fridge about half an hour before you want to start cooking.
Pre-heat the oven to 170°C., bake for an hour and 15 minutes with the foil on and for 15 minutes with the foil off. Serve hot.

Frittata

We first ate this whilst on holiday in Italy and liked it so much that we created our own version to make at home. It's similar to a Spanish tortilla (I just use sliced onions, gently fried till soft and sweet and sliced potatoes for that variation) and is lovely hot but can be eaten just warm as part of a picnic lunch.

Serves 2 - good with a side salad for a lunch or supper
Equipment: medium non-stick frying pan about 20cm in diameter
Takes: 10 minutes

Ingredients

5 eggs
A knob of butter
A pinch of sea salt

A pinch of English mustard powder
One small chopped onion
Base: either cooked cold chopped leftover potato, rice or freshly cooked pasta such as spaghetti or macaroni – enough to cover the base of the frying pan.
Toppings: chopped chorizo or ham, chopped herbs (parsley or chives work best), grated cheddar cheese or crumbled feta, grated courgettes, 2 tomatoes sliced.

Pre-heat the grill.
Heat a small knob of butter in the pan on the hob - medium heat.
Meanwhile, lightly beat the eggs, a pinch of sea salt and a pinch of English mustard powder in a bowl with a fork.
Once the hot butter is foaming, add and lightly sauté the chopped onion.
Add in and lightly sauté any other additional ingredients such as chopped ham or chorizo and whatever the base ingredient is – rice, potato or pasta.
Pour the egg mixture into the pan and let it settle into any spaces.
Let the bottom set slightly, layer your additional ingredients on top – cheese and sliced tomato.
Pop under the grill until the cheese and tomato topping is bubbling and the egg is set.
Turn out of the pan, cut into slices, serve and eat straightaway.

Nina's Favourite Banana Porridge

You can of course just eat plain porridge and follow the instructions on the pack but this makes a really yummy and sustaining alternative. A bowl of this in the morning can keep you going till lunchtime because of the slow release energy in oats. Using whole milk is a great way to get kids to eat something that's really good for them – full of calcium for healthy bones and teeth. If you're watching your weight, plain water, semi-skimmed or skimmed milk makes perfectly tasty porridge.

I use a tea or coffee mug to measure out the amount we like – about 50g is the average serving weight of the ready made sachets. I prefer the thicker rolled oats like Scott's Porage Oats or Sainsbury's 'Taste the difference' brand (farmer's markets are often a good source of organic oatmeal). Quaker Oats is a finer rolled blend and makes a smoother porridge, I prefer a bit of texture.

Serves 2

Equipment: non stick milk pan
Takes: 6 to 8 minutes

Ingredients
2 bananas, peeled and mashed
1 mug porridge oats
2 mugs semi-skimmed milk
2 teaspoons of Demerara sugar or home made vanilla or cinnamon sugar (see French Toast for the recipe)
A pinch of cinnamon

Mix the milk and oats together and cook gently in the milk pan on a low heat on the hob as per the instructions on the packet – roughly 8 minutes until it goes lovely and creamy. You can microwave it but all microwaving seems to rob food of its flavour somehow - stovetop cooking gives the best result. Soaking the oats overnight in some water and then cooking with a little extra milk makes it creamy and has fewer calories.
Place half the mashed banana in the base of each serving bowl.
Pour the hot porridge over the banana.
Sprinkle with sugar and dust with cinnamon.
Serve straightway with a dash of cream if you like.

Breakfast Banana Brûlée
This is a real treat on a Sunday morning, especially if you want a change from eggs and bacon but still want something a bit special to eat at the weekend.

Serves 4
Preheat the grill to high
Equipment: 4 ramekin dishes, a baking tray, small non-stick saucepan
Takes: 20 minutes

Ingredients
250 ml water
Pinch of sea salt
2 tablespoons of single cream
85g jumbo oats

2 teaspoons of ground cinnamon
4 teaspoons of brown sugar
1 tablespoon of caster sugar
1 tablespoon of toasted sunflower seeds
2 bananas, peeled and thinly sliced
300g whole milk yoghurt

Preheat the grill to high.
Bring the water and sea salt to the boil in the saucepan.
Stir in the oats and reduce the heat to low. Stir for 3-5 minutes or until the oats absorb the water.
Stir in the cream, cinnamon, sunflower seeds, and caster sugar.
Lightly butter the ramekin dishes.
Place an equal amount of the oat mixture into each ramekin.
Top the oats in each ramekin with a layer of sliced banana and then top each one with a quarter of the yogurt.
Sprinkle evenly with brown sugar and place the ramekins on the baking tray under the hot grill. It will take about a minute for the sugar to caramelise the sugar.
Remove from the grill.
They can be served warm or be refrigerated and served cold.

Home Made Yogurt

This is easy and really inexpensive to make yourself and tastes better than almost any shop bought yoghurt. You can then use it for a variety of basics - for breakfast, dessert, savoury dips or smoothies.

You will need a yoghurt maker from a kitchen store such as Lakeland. It costs about £20 for a container and the electric heating unit - it looks a bit like a baby's bottle warmer.

Ingredients
1 pint of full fat UHT milk (it must be UHT), I prefer to use the 'Moo' brand if I can.
1 tablespoon of live yoghurt – this is only required for your first batch. Rachel's Organic yoghurt is good one to use. Subsequent batches use the same amount of your existing yoghurt culture.
Optional – pinch of sea salt if you're using it for savoury dishes

Mix the live yoghurt starter, UHT milk and sea salt in the yoghurt pot. Place into the warmer, plug it in and leave it overnight (about 8 hours). In the morning you will have a pint container of delicious yoghurt. Leave it in the fridge to chill.

For a thicker version, stand a large fine sieve lined with a muslin cloth over a large bowl, pour in the yoghurt mixture and leave to drain for an hour or so. Throw away the thin yellowish liquid that drains into the bowl. Turn the thick yoghurt from the muslin into the bowl, scraping off anything that clings to the muslin with a rubber spatula.

Refrigerate and use as and when you need it – save a spoonful to start your next batch.

Variation

You can pour your yoghurt into a clean muslin cloth, tie it up and then suspend it over a bowl to allow the water to drip out. This creates a thick white type of cheese that Middle Eastern cooks call 'Labneh'. It's delicious sprinkled with sea salt and roasted, ground cumin and served with Middle Eastern food such as roast lamb, couscous and salads.

Golden Granola

This is a really simple breakfast cereal staple and more delicious and cheaper than anything you can buy in a supermarket or eateries like Prêt. A big tub full like this is enough for one person to eat 2 tablespoons of every day for about two weeks. I used to take it into to work and keep it in the canteen kitchen to eat. It kept disappearing though so I resorted to daily helpings in a Lock & Lock plastic pot instead.

Makes enough to fill a 2-litre plastic ice cream tub.
Preheat the oven to 140º C
Equipment: A large mixing bowl, 2 baking trays and enough baking parchment to cover both baking trays
Takes: 10 minutes to prepare, 2 hours to cook

Ingredients

4 tablespoons of sunflower oil
2 tablespoons of runny honey
2 tablespoons of light muscovado sugar

2 tablespoons of fruit juice – lemon, apple or pineapple juice work well

300g Jumbo oats. You could substitute spelt or wheat flakes for some of the oats to ring the changes

120g chopped nuts – almonds, hazelnuts, walnuts, pecans, pistachios - whatever you prefer

1 heaped teaspoon of ground cinnamon

A couple of pinches of sea salt

200g mixed dried fruit such as sour cherries, chopped dried apricot, chopped dates, golden sultanas and raisins

Mix all the ingredients together thoroughly in the mixing bowl except the dried fruit.

Place a sheet of the baking parchment onto each of the baking trays.

Lay half of the granola mixture on each baking sheet and spread it out flat and even.

Place the trays on the oven and allow it to toast very, very slowly for up to a couple of hours.

Check it occasionally to ensure that it is cooking evenly and not burning. It will smell heavenly!

Once it looks nice and golden, remove from the oven and leave it cool.

Depending on how good your oven is, you may find that the top tray cooks more quickly than the bottom one. If that's the case, take the top one out, move the second one up and leave for a few minutes longer until it's golden too.

Once cooled, place in an airtight plastic box (a clean, empty, two litre plastic ice cream carton is just the right size) and mix in the dried fruit.

Serve sprinkled on a dish of fruit (stewed, compote or sliced banana, grapes, strawberries etc.) and a serving of home made or bought Greek-style yoghurt.

'Super food' Commuter Muesli

Some people go to work on an egg, but this Bircher-style muesli based breakfast is my healthy 'super foods' choice for when I get to my desk in the morning. It keeps me going until lunchtime without the need to snack! I make up a big batch and keep it in an airtight plastic container and it lasts about a fortnight. It's less calories and effort to make than Golden Granola and it's nice to alternate.

I usually make this the night before and put it in the fridge so it's ready to take away on my way to work and the oats turn lovely and creamy.

You can add in any leftover nuts and dried fruit you may have bought for other recipes, especially at Christmas. Ring the changes and add other dried fruit that you may like such as dried sour cherries or sultanas. You don't need to add any sugar.

Ingredients

500g Jumbo oats I buy local organic ones from my local farmers market but any conservation grade or organic ones will do.
100g chopped dried apricots, dates or prunes
100g pumpkin seeds
150g chopped nuts - almonds, hazelnuts, pecans etc.

Weigh out the ingredients into a large bowl. Mix them up so the nuts and dried fruit are evenly distributed. Pour into an airtight container and use as required.

To serve: Add 3 tablespoons (about 50g) to a cereal bowl or a Lock & Lock spill-proof plastic container if you're eating on the go. Then, add as much of your favourite fruit juice or coconut water as you need (about 50 to 100ml) to the mix to moisten and plump out the dried fruit and grains. Top it off with a tablespoon of Greek yoghurt and your favourite fresh fruit or compote. If I have time, I add freshly grated apple. If not, a handful of fresh berries - blueberries or raspberries are my 'fast favourites'.

Smoothies

Who needs cartons of shop bought smoothies when you have a blender and bowl of fruit? Admittedly, there is the washing up! These are often marketed as health foods but they contain quite a lot of calories, as they are full of fruit sugar, so you probably wouldn't want to drink too many every week. Veggie juicers are good alternative if you have a proper juicer like a Nutribullett.

Serves 2
Equipment: A blender or smoothie maker
Takes: 10 minutes

Basically, all you do is just throw your preferred fruit combinations into the blender, blitz and serve. It's a great quick breakfast or snack, just remember to leave the blender soaking in some water if you don't wash up right away or it will be a royal pain to clean up later.

Ripe fruit, especially bananas (the skins should be spotted brown) are essential for really good flavour. Any fruit that's likely to get left in the fruit bowl can be experimented with really rather than letting it go to waste – it's a good way to stumble upon a new favourite. If you've made your own yoghurt, they'll be even cheaper and tastier. Add a drop of good quality vanilla or almond essence for an extra flavour dimension, throw in a bit of fine oatmeal to make a 'thickie'.

Pigeon Cottage Favourite Combos

Plain Banana – 2 large overripe bananas, 250ml natural yoghurt, a drop of vanilla essence and an ice cube.
Banana and Orange – 3 ripe bananas, 250ml natural yoghurt, the juice of one large orange.
Strawberry & Banana – 6 to 8 strawberries, a ripe banana, 100ml natural yoghurt, 4 ice cubes.
Nectarine, Banana and Raspberry – 1 stoned, ripe nectarine, 1 banana, a handful of raspberries, 3 ice cubes, a little water to thin it down.
Pineapple and Banana – a quarter of fresh pineapple, 1 banana, 4 ice cubes, the juice of a large orange.

CHAPTER TWO: SOUP

> "Worries go down better with soup".
> Jewish Proverb

Warming, nutritious, comforting, quick and delicious – what's not to like about soup? You can make soup out of just about anything, so experimentation is the order of the day as is using seasonal vegetables that will be cheaper and have more flavour anyway. If you have an organic or seasonal veg box delivered, you can mix it up with whatever arrives in your delivery. The measures in these recipes are approximate - make things how you like them. With a few vegetables and a bit of imagination you can produce a delicious family sized pan of soup for a fraction of the price of shop bought cartons. If you buy a decent quality wide neck soup flask it can easily be added to a winter school or work lunch box. My Dad always takes his with him when he goes for day out fishing.

There aren't too many rules about cooking a good, hearty soup so anyone can make a decent job of it really. Just don't boil the backside off it, remember to let it cool a little before adding cream so it doesn't curdle and avoid adding so much as to drown the flavour of the other ingredients. Don't be tempted to use flour as a thickening as that too can deaden the flavour.

Using Stock

The basis of most well flavoured soups, sauces and risottos is the stock. Restaurants make professional stocks every day. Busy home cooks can easily use gel stockpots, stock cubes or powder and still get good results. My favourites for soup are Knorr gel pots or Marigold vegetable stock powder. Just remember not to add any more seasoning until the end in case it becomes too salty. Try it once it's ready and, if you still think it needs more sea salt or pepper, just add it to taste before serving.

If you've boiled a ham (see my recipe in Chapter Three), you can always reserve the stock and freeze it to use in soups or risottos. You can make a good white chicken stock by cooking up some chicken wings and vegetables such as onion, carrot and celery with some parsley stalks. 'Pour and Store' plastic bags are perfect for freezing stock or soup for later use.

Soup Essentials - Soffrito or Mirepoix

The key technique for making a good soup base is to make what the Italians call a soffrito and the French call a mirepoix. Peel and finely chop a potato, an onion and a stick of celery for a white base (you can add a carrot for a deeper flavour but it changes the colour of the soup obviously), melt a decent dollop of butter in a large saucepan and then very gently, sweat the vegetables for about 8 minutes. Next, make a **cartouche** by tearing off a square of baking parchment, fold it in half three times and then roughly tear a rounded edge on the outer edge so that, when you open it, it forms a circle. Lay it on top of the vegetables and scrunch it down around the edges. The combination of cooking in a mixture of steam and butter really brings out the flavour of the vegetables and then you can use it as the base for any number of soups.

These soup recipes are usually enough to feed four generously, especially if they're served with a nice hunk of crusty bread.

Leek and Potato Soup

Peel and dice a couple of medium sized potatoes and clean and slice a couple of nice thick leeks. Melt a large knob of butter and a dash of olive oil in a wide based, deep pan. Add the vegetables, stir and gently sweat them under a parchment cartouche (see above) for about 8 minutes. Add a pint of chicken stock and cook for about 10 minutes, season to taste.

To serve: for a rustic soup, mash the vegetables in the pan with a potato masher, add a handful of chopped fresh herbs like chives or parsley and a swirl of cream. For a more elegant soup, blend the lot with a hand held blender until smooth.

Chicken Soup

Peel and finely chop an onion, a stick of celery, a leek and/or a carrot. Melt a knob of butter in saucepan, gently sweat the vegetables under a cartouche and add a pint of hot chicken stock. Cook for a further 10 minutes. **Variations** – liquidise the stock vegetables and the liquid and then add some chopped chicken meat. Cook for another 15 minutes. For **cream of chicken soup** add a dash of cream and seasoning before serving.

Adding a drained tin of sweet corn will give you a **chicken and sweet corn soup**.

To make **chicken noodle soup** just add a handful of broken vermicelli noodles at the same as you add the chicken.

For a **chunky chicken vegetable soup** add some more chopped vegetables such as carrots and potatoes and a few peas at the end. For **chicken mulligatawny soup** add a little hot curry paste and a handful of basmati rice.

For a **hot chicken and coconut soup** substitute a tin of coconut milk for the cream and add freshly chopped red chilli and some finely grated fresh ginger and/or some finely chopped fresh lemongrass root.

Roasted Vegetable Soup

If you oven roast a peeled and diced butternut squash, carrots, sweet potatoes or parsnips (make it with one of these or a mixture of all of them) with some butter, sea salt and pepper, then add a pint of hot chicken stock and blend it, you can make a thick and flavoursome soup. Season the soup with a touch of grated nutmeg, a teaspoon of ground mace or a smear of curry paste. Add a swirl of cream, crème fraiche or some crumbled feta cheese or chopped chives to garnish and add extra flavour.

Roasted Tomato Soup

Skin and halve about 900g of very ripe tomatoes, drizzle them with olive oil and a couple of cloves of crushed garlic, a dessert spoon of red wine vinegar, a little sea salt and roast them in a baking dish in a hot oven for about 40 minutes. Blend and then add a little hot water to thin. Pass through a metal sieve to make it smoother if needs be. Season and serve. Serve with an extra drizzle of olive oil, a dash of sherry or balsamic vinegar or some basil pesto. Alternatively, add a dash of cream to make velvety cream of tomato soup.

Yellow Split Pea Soup with Smoked Sausage
This yummy soup is inspired by a Nigella recipe I came across in her excellent book 'Feast'.

Peel and chop an onion, 2 carrots, a clove of garlic and a stick of celery and blitz it in a food processor. Heat a couple of tablespoons of vegetable or light olive oil in a large saucepan, add the vegetable mix and cook gently for 10 minutes until soft. Add and stir in half a teaspoon of freshly ground mace (the magic ingredient – don't make it without the mace) and then add in 500g of rinsed yellow split peas and stir together thoroughly. Add 1.5 litres of hot vegetable stock made with Marigold powder (or chicken stock made with a Kallo cube) and 2 fresh bay leaves. Cook for an hour until everything is soft and cooked adding more stock if it becomes too thick and stodgy. Make it smooth with a hand held blender if you want a silkier textured soup. Season with sea salt, a dash more ground mace and add in sliced coins of smoked sausage – I use Matheson's or German Frankfurters from the deli. You could also substitute leftover chunks of cooked ham.

Lentil & Ham Soup
I like to make this lentil soup when I've cooked a gammon ham (or a ham hock) so that I can use the stock and add some shredded cold ham.

Rinse 250g of green lentils and then cover them with a couple of pints of cold water with a vegetable stock cube or your leftover ham stock. Add in a peeled chopped onion and a stick of celery; bring the pot to the boil and then turn down the heat to simmer for about 15 minutes. Liquidise the lentils with the vegetables, taste and adjust the seasoning. Serve with a sprinkling of chunky chopped cold ham.

Fresh Green Pea & Ham Soup
Use the stock from a boiled ham hock or gammon – about a litre and a half and reserve some of the shredded meat to serve. Melt 25g of butter in a

saucepan and gently sauté a couple of banana shallots and a clove of garlic and a couple of rashers of unsmoked chopped bacon. Don't let the shallot brown, just cook until it's translucent and gives up its sweetness. Add the stock, another large knob of butter and 800g of frozen petits pois (defrost another 100g to serve). Warm through and then liquidise. Pass through a sieve to get a more velvety texture and season with sea salt and ground white pepper to taste. Warm the soup before serving, ladle into a bowl and garnish each bowl with shredded ham and fresh peas.

Optional: Heston's mint oil. Drop 25g of fresh mint leaves into boiling water for 20 seconds. Drain and then put them into iced water to stop them cooking any further. Then dry them with some kitchen paper. Blend the mint leaves and 100g of groundnut oil in a liquidizer, strain and pour into a bottle. It keeps for up to 4 days in the fridge. Use as a garnish for the soup or to dress roasted vegetables or a salad.

Fresh Pea & Roasted Garlic Soup

This is definitely good enough for a dinner party starter or a 'get the girls round' lunch. It doesn't take long but you need to roast a whole head of fresh garlic first of all which takes a good hour. Don't worry about peeling the garlic, just slice it in half horizontally and drizzle it with some olive oil. Put the two halves back together and then loosely wrap it in a parcel of baking foil and bake it on a tray in a preheated oven at 200°C for an hour. Add 200g of frozen peas to 100ml of warm chicken stock, a large knob of butter, 2 tablespoons of grated Parmesan and squeeze in the roasted cloves of garlic to a blender and liquidise. Pass it through a sieve to make it a nice velvety texture and then add another 100ml of chicken stock. Warm it gently, season to taste and stir in a tablespoon of double cream.

Celeriac Soup

This is another soup that's good enough for a dinner party starter. Melt a large knob of butter in a pan and cook a large peeled and chopped head of celeriac, a shredded leek, a medium chopped onion and a crushed clove of garlic gently for five minutes. Add a litre of chicken, ham or vegetable stock and the juice of a lemon (to stop the celeriac going brown and to add a little acidity to the flavour) and simmer gently until the vegetables are cooked.

Blend in the pan with a hand held blender, until smooth. Add a half a litre of milk if you want a creamier soup and then season with salt and ground white pepper. Serve hot or chilled. Garnish with freshly chopped parsley or chive flowers and snipped leaves to make it look extra special.

Onion Soup with Cheese Topped Croutons

Melt a generous knob of butter and a couple of tablespoons of olive oil in a saucepan and then add 6 large and finely sliced onions and 3 peeled, crushed cloves of garlic. Season with some salt and pepper, cover and cook very gently on a low heat for about 45 minutes or until the onions are soft and caramelised. Stir them from time to time to stop them from sticking to the bottom of the pan. Then add 1.5 litres of good quality hot beef stock – either stock leftover from a pot roast like a brisket or use a tub of ready made stock. I have used tins of beef consommé as a cheat in the past quite successfully! Cook for another 15 minutes and then add 2 tablespoons of Madeira for the last 10 minutes. Adjust the seasoning to taste.

Cut enough slices for the number of people you are serving from a white bloomer/French loaf; brown both sides under a hot grill and then cover them with a smearing of Dijon mustard and grated cheddar (you can add Gruyère cheese of course but it's tricky eating all that melted and stringy cheese with any decorum!). Put them back under the grill to melt the cheese. Ladle the onion soup into individual soup bowls and then put the giant crouton on top once the cheese is bubbly and melting. Yum.

Smoked Haddock Chowder

This has to be my all time favourite soup. I had my best ever bowl of this in an old fisherman's pub on the Northumberland coast one New Year after a freezing cold walk up the beach with friends, kids and dogs. It certainly brought life back to my frozen limbs. Happy days!

Ingredients
2 tablespoons of olive oil
2 tablespoons of butter
2 finely chopped onions
2 quartered and finely sliced leeks

3 stalks of de-strung and finely chopped celery
6 medium sized potatoes, peeled and diced
3 cloves of garlic crushed with 1 teaspoon of sea salt
2 teaspoons of chopped fresh thyme
Freshly chopped parsley
1 pint of milk
2 decent sized pieces of haddock, cooked in a pint of water seasoned with a bay leaf (reserve the stock)

Heat the oil and butter in large pan. Add the garlic, onions, leeks, celery and potatoes and cook gently for 5 minutes – colour but don't brown. Stir in the thyme, the smoked haddock stock and bring to the boil. Reduce the heat and simmer for ten minutes until the vegetables have cooked. Take out half the soup and mash it with a potato masher. Return it to the pan along with the milk and the flaked smoked haddock. Simmer for 3 minutes, season and serve with a garnish of chopped fresh parsley.

College Soup

I call this College Soup or Uni-strone (it is essentially a Minestrone soup) because I used to live on big fat bowls of this when I was a (very) poor student. I still love it but I can afford to make it with slightly nicer ingredients these days! You can make this soup at any time of year with whatever seasonal vegetables are available. I always use the ham stock leftover from cooking a gammon but you could use chicken stock as well. The really special ingredient is the addition of a leftover rind from a piece of Parmesan (never throw that bit away however gross it looks!) – it adds a lovely depth of flavour. This will serve six people quite easily. Eaten with some crusty bread, it is a meal on its own.

Pre-soak about 200g of borlotti or white beans such as cannellini the night before (you can used tinned if speed is of the essence but they aren't quite as nice or as inexpensive), and cook them according to the instructions on the pack. They may need rapid boiling for about 20 minutes before you eat them as some dried beans contain a toxin that can be poisonous if they aren't boiled.

In a large pan on the hob, gently sweat four chopped slices of pancetta or bacon and couple of chopped celery sticks, 2 carrots, 2 onions, 2 garlic cloves and a chopped head of fennel in some olive oil for about 20 minutes. Add two large tins of chopped plum tomatoes, 2 chopped courgettes, a glass of red wine, the Parmesan rind, the beans, the stock and a handful of dried pasta. You can use spaghetti broken into short pieces, vermicelli or tiny ditalini pasta. Cook it through for about 15 more minutes; add some chopped French string beans or fresh peas just before serving and some torn up basil leaves. Serve with a drizzle of olive oil and a grating of fresh Parmesan cheese. Delish!

WHAT'S4TEAMUM?

CHAPTER THREE: MEAT MAIN COURSES

"My favourite animal is steak".
Fran Lebowitz
(American author – the modern day Dorothy Parker)

If I fancy 'eating fancy' with exotic ingredients, flavoured foams and arty smears or dots of weird purées and gels 'Masterchef' style, then I go to a decent restaurant. Life's too short to bother to cook that type of food at home. These recipes are the ones that we like to eat with friends and family. - dinner parties don't need to be stressful. All you need to do is just serve everything on attractive china, throw in some decent napkins and the addition of a few nicer garnishes than you would for a weekday! If it tastes good, everyone will happy. For the pickier guest, simply top up their wine glass more often. That way either they won't care, or won't remember, what they ate.

Meat Matters
I couldn't afford to buy a lot of meat when I first started cooking, but I did learn to treat it with respect. So, here are my tops tips.

1. Buy the **best quality meat** you can afford. Eat less rather than consume inferior, tough or tasteless meat. The better the animal was fed and treated in life, the better it tastes when cooked.
2. Preferably, always buy it from a **reputable local butcher** rather than a supermarket. My local butcher, Mr Hubbard, is a real treasure and he knows everything about the provenance of the meat and the best cuts for every method of cooking.
3. Buy with your eye. **Properly hung beef** should be dark red not bright red. Fat should be cream coloured not white. Beef that is marbled with fat will be more succulent and will 'disappear' in the cooking process thereby creating FLAVOUR.
4. Buy **whole pieces** of meat such as shin or shoulder for casseroles and cut it yourself so all the pieces are the same size. That way, it should cook evenly.
5. Never try to cook meat straight from the **fridge** – always bring it up to

room temperature or it will shrink more, or be cooked on the outside and raw inside.
6. Always allow joints of beef, pork, chicken and lamb to **rest** for at least 20 minutes before carving – it will be easier to carve and taste much better.
7. When **browning meat**, just cook a few pieces in the pan at a time or it will steam and turn grey not golden brown.
8. Use **cheaper cuts** of chicken such as thigh meat for curries and casseroles – less cost, more flavour.
9. Cheaper cuts such as oxtail, pork or ox cheeks have great flavour but need **long, slow cooking** to deliver tenderness. Any good butcher will order them in for you if you ask.
10. **Fat means flavour** – cut the fat off a chop or spoon fat off a casserole *after* it has cooked not before or it won't taste of very much.
11. Ask your butcher for a chunk of **marrowbone** to add to casseroles or for roasting joints on - it will add great flavour and they don't usually charge you for them.
12. Make good meat in e.g. stews **go further** by adding lots of tasty vegetables or pulses.

Mel's Diner Chilli Con Carne

The cumin-flavoured chilli we ate in San Francisco at the original Mel's diner used in the film classic, American Graffiti, inspires this recipe. Serve with guacamole and/or sour cream, rice or Matzo crackers.

Serves 4
Can be cooked on the hob and finished off in the oven.
Equipment: oven proof or cast iron casserole that can also be used on the hob or a saucepan.
Takes: 20 minutes preparation, plus 90 minutes to 2 hours or so to cook through.

Ingredients
500g minced beef or cubed stewing beef
1 400g tin of chopped tomatoes
1 400g tin of red kidney, black or borlotti beans, drained and rinsed
2 tablespoons of tomato puree

1 square of e.g. Green & Black's quality 80% dark chocolate – optional but adds a lovely depth and shine to the final result
1 tablespoon of olive oil
1 tablespoon of ground cumin
2 bay leaves
1 fresh green chilli deseeded and chopped, a quarter of a teaspoon of dried red chilli flakes and a teaspoon of cayenne pepper – add more or less depending on how hot you like it.
1 onion, finely chopped
2 fat cloves of garlic
Sea salt and freshly milled black pepper

Finely chop the onions and garlic.
Heat the oil in whichever pan you are using.
Add the onion and garlic to the oil and cook gently for about 5 minutes until softened.
Turn up the heat, add the minced beef and stir until nicely browned, then add and fry in the ground cumin. If you use cubed beef, brown it in batches so you can get a nice caramelised crust on it.
Add the tinned tomatoes, tomato puree, chilli, bay leaves, sea salt and pepper.
Stir and either leave to simmer gently on the hob for 40 minutes until the meat is tender and the sauce is nice and thick, or put the lid on to your casserole and leave in the oven for a couple of hours or more at about 150°C. It is much nicer finished in the oven.
Add the beans about 10 minutes before you want to serve it just to warm them through.
Remove from the hob or oven.
Check the seasoning to taste before serving.

Guacamole

Served at many a birthday lunch party with chilli, fajitas or tortilla chips, this is the most awesome guacamole ever according to Nina's friend Sarah. This should serve 6 people easily as an accompaniment and needs to be made shortly before you want to serve it because it doesn't keep that well. The lime juice stops the avocado from going brown and sludgy as well as giving it that sharp Mexican-style flavour. Some recipes for this include chopped, skinned tomato or chopped red onion although I prefer to keep it pure and green. The recipe is scaled so there's three of everything so it's easy to scale up or down in terms of quantity, although it's hardly worth making with less than two avocados.

Ingredients
3 absolutely ripe avocados
Juice of 3 limes
½ finely chopped and deseeded fresh green chilli
A good pinch of sea salt
3 finely sliced spring onions or half a finely chopped red onion for a splash of colour
3 tablespoons of chopped fresh coriander for preference. Flat leaf parsley is OK but not as nice. Lovage makes an interesting addition if you have it growing in your garden.

Chop and quickly mix the avocados in a bowl leaving it slightly chunky in texture. Dissolve the sea salt in the lime juice and then mix into the avocado mixture along with the finely chopped spring onion and coriander. Check for seasoning and serve immediately.

Pigeon Cottage Pie

Comforting and tasty, this is everyone's favourite winter supper. Serve with either some lightly cooked, shredded spring greens or peas. My favourite is to serve it with pickled red cabbage (preferably home made or Garner's brand if shop bought), my Pigeon Cottage plum ketchup or a dash of HP brown sauce on the side. For an extra special twist, mix in a steamed, diced head of celeriac with the mash topping.

Serves 4
Equipment: ovenproof dish and 2 saucepans
Takes: 30 minutes preparation, plus 25 minutes or so to cook through. Cooks on the hob and is finished off in the oven

Ingredients
600g of good quality minced beef
1 tablespoon sunflower oil
1 large onion, finely chopped
1 carrot, finely chopped
1 stick of celery, finely chopped

1 finely chopped and shredded leek (adds a lovely texture and flavour)
Sea salt and freshly milled black pepper
¼ pint hot rich beef stock
1 tablespoon of plain flour
A couple of shakes of Worcestershire sauce and light soya sauce
Optional cheat: replace the flour with 2 dessertspoons of Bisto gravy granules to thicken it
5 or 6 large potatoes, peeled and cut into evenly sized pieces
Small head of celeriac (optional) – peeled, cubed and set aside in water with a dash of lemon juice to stop it from browning
2 tablespoons of milk
1 knob of butter and a little extra for the topping
Grated Cheddar for the topping (optional)

Peel the potatoes and cut into evenly sized pieces. Place in a saucepan and cover with boiling water and a pinch of sea salt. Simmer and cook until tender for about 20 minutes.

In another pan of boiling water, cook the cubed celeriac if using, drain, let the steam evaporate and then add to the mashed potato.

Meanwhile, finely chop the onions, carrot, celery and leek.

Heat the oil in a pan on the hob.

Add the vegetables to the oil and cook gently for about 5 minutes until softened.

Turn up the heat, add the minced beef and stir until nicely browned.

Stir in the flour and cook for a moment or two.

Season with freshly milled black pepper.

Add the hot stock so it just comes to the same level as the meat mixture.

Or, stir in the Bisto granules until the gravy thickens – add more to taste if necessary.

Add a couple of shakes of Worcestershire sauce and/or soya sauce.

Pre-heat the oven to 200°C.

Leave the meat sauce to cook gently for about 25 minutes on the hob until the meat is tender and the sauce is nice and thick – you want the mash to sit on top not sink through it. Check the seasoning to taste and then turn it into your baking dish.

By this time, your potatoes should be cooked. Drain them, leave them a few minutes to allow the steam to evaporate. Mash with the milk and butter until lump free but not so smooth that it will dissolve into the meat mixture in the oven. (mash and cream in the celeriac if using)

Carefully spoon the potato on to the top of the thick meat sauce, dab a little butter on the top (grated cheese is also yummy) and pop it in the oven for about 25 minutes.

Once the top is golden, take it out of the oven and leave it to rest for a few minutes before serving.

Pigeon Cottage Meat Loaf

A delicious and simple to make family supper dish, this is great with mashed potato and green vegetables, or a tomato sauce and noodles.

Serves 4
Pre-heat the oven to 180°C
Equipment: Greased loaf tin, frying pan and a mixing bowl, small food processor
Takes: 10 minutes preparation, plus 40 minutes or so to cook through

Ingredients

600g of minced meat – beef or pork or lamb
1 tablespoon sunflower oil
1 large onion, finely chopped
1 stick of celery, finely chopped
1 carrot, grated (optional)
2 slices of white or wholemeal bread with the crusts removed and make into fine breadcrumbs in a small food processor
1 egg, beaten
Sea salt and freshly milled black pepper
A couple of shakes of Worcestershire sauce
1 level tablespoon of dried oregano (or mint if using lamb)

Pre-heat the oven to 180°C.
Finely chop the onions, carrots and celery.
Heat the oil in the pan.
Add the onion and celery to the oil and cook gently for about 5 minutes until softened. Add in and gently cook the carrots if you're using them. This seals in the flavour and juices.
Put the minced meat in the mixing bowl with the dried oregano and the

beaten egg.
Season with freshly milled black pepper and a little sea salt and a shake or two of Worcestershire sauce. (I like a dash of plum ketchup in the pork version).
Make the breadcrumbs and add to the mixture.
Stir it all together and spoon into the greased loaf tin. Pat it down gently so that it is level with the top of the tin.
Place in the oven and leave to cook for about 40 minutes until the crust is brown.
Take it out of the oven, leave to rest for 5 minutes or so before turning out on to a plate. Cut into thick slices and serve. You could spoon some gravy over it or a little of the home made tomato sauce in the next recipe.

Magnificent Meatballs

I regularly ate a very similar dish to this when I worked a gap year summer as an English teacher in Greece. This recipe is adapted from a Jamie Oliver style Italian version that I particularly like and I've shown the options for the Greek alternative in brackets.

Serves 4 – 6
Pre-heat the oven to 200°C
Equipment: Rectangular baking dish. Mixing bowl, saucepan
Takes: 20 minutes preparation, plus 40 minutes or so to cook through

Ingredients
700g minced beef
4 tablespoons olive oil
1 large onion, finely chopped
1 clove of garlic, crushed and chopped
1 level tablespoon Dijon mustard (replace this with a tablespoon of ouzo for the Greek version)
2 slices of white or wholemeal bread with the crusts removed and make into fine breadcrumbs in a small food processor
1 egg yolk, beaten
Sea salt and freshly ground black pepper
2 level dessertspoons of dried oregano
½ teaspoon ground cumin (omit for the Greek version)

½ teaspoon dried red chilli flakes
1 tablespoon finely chopped fresh rosemary
A handful of fresh basil, torn (omit in the Greek version)
60g mozzarella cheese, torn into pieces (replace the mozzarella and parmesan with feta for the Greek version)
60g Parmesan cheese
1 quantity of tomato sauce
Serve with a green salad on the side, some pasta noodles, crusty bread or rice

Pre-heat the oven to 200°C.
The tomato sauce takes an hour so start that first.
Finely chop the onions and garlic.
Heat the oil in the pan.
Add the onion and garlic to the oil and cook gently for about 5 minutes until softened and then let them cool.
Put the minced meat in the mixing bowl with the dried oregano, cumin, red chilli, chopped rosemary and the beaten egg.
Season with freshly milled black pepper and a little sea salt.
Make the breadcrumbs and add to the mixture with the cooled onions, garlic and the mustard.
Stir it all together and then, with wet hands, roll and pat into meatballs the size and shape you want.
Place them in a buttered baking dish, cover with the tomato sauce, mozzarella and basil. Sprinkle the Parmesan on top. You can fry the meatballs lightly beforehand, although I don't bother and it tastes just as nice with the tops just browned from being in the oven.
Place in the oven and leave to cook for about 25 minutes until the cheese is golden.
Take it out of the oven, leave to rest and cool slightly for 5 minutes or so before serving or you'll end up with a burnt mouth.

Tomato Sauce for Meatballs & Meatloaf Recipe
This is a really versatile recipe and can be used with lots of different dishes. Sometimes, I make a big batch and freeze what I don't need so I have it ready for quick midweek suppers.
Cook on the hob
Equipment: Thick bottomed, broad based pan

Takes: 10 minutes prep, cooks for 1 hour

Ingredients
1 large clove of garlic, crushed and finely chopped
3 tablespoons olive oil
1/2 teaspoon red chilli flakes
2 teaspoons dried oregano (add fresh too if you have it – I grow it in my garden very easily in the summer)
1 400g tin of chopped plum tomatoes
Optional: two or three finely chopped Sunblush tomatoes
1 tablespoon red wine vinegar (you can add red wine but the vinegar is cheaper and tastier)
Sea salt and ground black pepper to taste

Gently fry the garlic with the oil.
Add the chilli, oregano and the tomatoes.
Mix gently and bring to the boil and gently simmer for about an hour. Add the vinegar, break up the tomatoes a little if necessary and add the rest of the olive oil. Season well to taste and add the fresh herbs.
Add to the pasta or meatballs as appropriate.

Simply Sausages
There are only two things you need to know about sausages. Always buy a good quality butcher's sausage and never prick them before you cook them or they will go dry.
You can cook them on the grill, gently fry them, oven roast or braise them. When oven roasting them, just put a little sunflower oil in the roasting tin so that they don't stick and season them with some finely ground black pepper. Serve with my recipes for creamy mash and onion gravy, Yorkshire pudding and your favourite vegetables or serve with savoury lentils.

'Sausage Daisy'
This was always a bit of a favourite with Nina's friends when they came round for tea after school. It's not a recipe, just a way of making something everyday a bit more interesting and a good way to get kids to eat broccoli! Carefully place a mound of fluffy mashed potatoes in the middle of each

dinner plate, cut 2 cooked sausages per person in half and arrange them at 12, 3, 6 and 9 o'clock around the plate with the cut ends against the mash. Between each piece of sausage, lay a floret of broccoli with the stalk side into the mash. It looks like a weird daisy! Serve with a jug of gravy so they can help themselves, or ketchup if requested. Simple pleasures!

Cocktail Party Sausages

Chipolata size sausages coated with a mixture of a tablespoon of honey and whole grain mustard, or honey and soy sauce, are great roasted in the oven for about 30 minutes in a hot oven. They always go down well at a drinks party and are usually wolfed down in great quantities at the infamous Pigeon Cottage Christmas quiz party.

Toad in the Hole

Meaty sausages cooked in a Yorkshire pudding with gravy and/or mash – heavenly! I took a long time to get around cooking this regularly because I thought it was too much trouble to make unless it was for a lot of people but it really is so easy to cook a small version or individual portions and kids love it. Make it with the roasted onion gravy and it will transform it to something beyond heavenly.

Serves 2 people – just scale up the quantities for more people
Equipment: Large Pyrex measuring jug or a bowl to make the batter, medium sized (23 x 15 cm) flameproof roasting dish for the toad (or a small roasting dish for individual portions), frying pan.
Takes: 25 minutes prep, 30 minutes to cook

Ingredients
6 good quality pork sausages from a butcher
75g plain flour
1 large egg
80ml milk and 20ml water
A really generous pinch of ground white pepper (not black as it makes the pudding look burnt) and a good pinch of sea salt
A knob of dripping or a tablespoon of cooking oil

Pre-heat the oven to 220°C.

Mix the egg, milk, sea salt and pepper together thoroughly in the jug or bowl with a whisk.

Allow this mixture to stand for 15 minutes and then whisk in the flour. The batter should be smooth and lump free.

Meanwhile brown and cook the sausages in for about 10 minutes a frying pan with a little oil so they don't stick.

Ensure the oven is hot at 220°C, add the oil to the baking dish and, once it's really smoking hot, add the sausages and then pour the pudding mixture in the tin all around the sausages. The batter should sizzle and crackle when you add it and that way it forms a nice crust and doesn't stick to the pan when you want to get it out.

Put it straight back into the oven on to the middle shelf so that once it rises it doesn't stick to the oven roof. Cook for 30 minutes until golden and risen. Don't open the oven door during cooking or it won't rise or will deflate.

Make the gravy and mash whilst the pudding is cooking.

Take it out of the oven when risen and golden and serve immediately.

Roasted Onion Gravy

This gravy is delicious with any meat dish where there isn't a lot of meat stock such as toad in the hole. This is based on a Delia recipe but I've changed the method because I think it's easier my way and it still tastes great.

Serves 4
Takes: 30 minutes
Equipment: frying pan

Ingredients

2 large onions, peeled and sliced
2 teaspoons sunflower oil
1 teaspoon of golden caster sugar
1 dessertspoon of Worcestershire sauce
1 teaspoon of mustard powder
1 dessertspoon of plain flour
425ml vegetable stock made from dissolving 1 1/2 teaspoons Marigold Swiss bouillon

powder dissolved in boiling water.
Sea salt and freshly ground black pepper

Place the chopped onions, oil and sugar in a frying pan and mix thoroughly. On a medium heat, gently brown and caramelise the onions for about 20 minutes.

When they are ready, stir in the flour and allow it to cook through for a couple of minutes.

Boil a kettle and make the stock with the Marigold powder, mustard and Worcestershire sauce.

Gradually add in the stock to the onion mix and stir until smooth. If serving this with chops or sausages, you can always deglaze the roasting pan with a little hot water and add the juices to the gravy for extra meaty flavour.

Bring to simmering point and cook for another 5 minutes. Add a little more water if it goes too thick. Taste to check the seasoning and pour into a warmed serving jug.

Braised Sausages with Beans

This is a great winter comfort food dish and was the very first dish my old commuter friend Bonnie cooked for me for lunch when she went on maternity leave. We used to joke all the time about what an 'Undomesticated Goddess' she was at the time, so she road tested this thoroughly on her husband before she made it for me. I really loved it, copied the recipe, and I've been making it ever since. Make it with pork or venison sausages.

Serves 2-3 people comfortably with mash and vegetables. For more just increase the number of sausages and vegetables.
Equipment: 2.25 litre flameproof, lidded casserole dish
Takes: 20 minutes prep, cook in the oven for 2 hours

Ingredients
6 good quality pork or venison sausages
1 400g tin of beans – cannellini or borlotti preferably, drained. You can make it with dried and soaked beans, it is nicer but it just depends how much time you have on your hands
1 heaped teaspoon of fresh rosemary and one of fresh chopped sage or thyme

Juniper berries – venison version only
110g sliced, smoked pancetta or bacon
1 tablespoon of olive oil
1 large onion, peeled and chopped
2 cloves of garlic, crushed
275ml dry white wine for pork sausages, red for the venison version
Sea salt and freshly ground black pepper

Pre-heat the oven to 150°C.
Heat the oil in the casserole on the hob and gently brown the sausages for about 8 minutes.
Remove the sausages and set aside on a plate.
Add the pancetta, fry until crisp, remove and place with the sausages.
Turn the heat to medium, add the onions and cook until softened for about 10 minutes, then add the garlic and cook for another minute or so.
Put the sausages, pancetta, beans, fresh herbs, sea salt, pepper and wine into the casserole and bring up to simmering point.
Put the lid on the casserole and cook slowly for two hours.
Serve with creamy mash and green vegetables.

Suffolk Cider Sausages

I used to make this in the autumn when there was a glut of windfall apples donated by my neighbour. It really doesn't need the apples though, so now I make it any time of the year with just the cider.
Serves 2-3 people comfortably with mash and veg. For more, just increase the number of sausages and vegetables.
Equipment: Flameproof, lidded casserole dish
Takes: 20 minutes prep, cook in the oven for 1 hour

Ingredients
6 good quality pork sausages
425 ml strong dry cider, Aspall's Suffolk vintage cider for preference
1 tablespoon of cider vinegar, Aspall's again
225g sliced, smoked pancetta or bacon
1 tablespoon of olive oil
1 large onion, peeled and chopped
2 cloves of garlic, crushed

A few sprigs of fresh thyme
1 tablespoon of plain flour
2 bay leaves
Sea salt and freshly ground black pepper

Pre-heat the oven to 150°C.
Heat the oil in the casserole on the hob and gently brown the sausages for about 8 minutes.
Remove the sausages and set aside on a plate.
Add the pancetta, fry until crisp, remove and place with the sausages.
Turn the heat to medium, add the onions and cook until softened for about 10 minutes, then add the garlic and cook for another minute or so.
Put the sausages, pancetta, sea salt, pepper and flour into the casserole, stir until absorbed and then add the cider, cider vinegar, bay leaves and thyme and bring up to simmering point.
Put the lid on the casserole and cook slowly for an hour.
Serve with creamy mash and green vegetables.

Puy Lentil & Smoked Sausage Supper

This is a ridiculously quick and tasty 'one pot' supper dish. It uses mostly store cupboard ingredients and is very useful for getting rid of those odds and ends of veg leftover in the fridge at the end of week.

Serves 2 to 3 people comfortably. For larger numbers, just scale up the number of sausages and vegetables.
Equipment: Thick bottomed, broad based pan
Takes: 10 minutes prep, cooks on the hob for 25 minutes

Ingredients
1 large clove of garlic, crushed and finely chopped
1 large finely chopped onion
4 carrots (2 per person), peeled and cut on the diagonal into 5 cm long chunks
2 potatoes, peeled and diced
2 sticks of celery (1 per person) cut on the diagonal into 5cm long chunks
A couple of rashers of streaky bacon or pancetta, chopped
1 smoked sausage (Matheson's or the nice German bratwurst kind), cut on the diagonal into 5cm long chunks or coins

120g Puy lentils, rinsed with water and drained
1 tablespoon of olive oil
6 chopped sundried or sunblush tomatoes
1/2 teaspoon red chilli flakes
Half a pint of hot water
A couple of fresh bay leaves and a couple of sprigs of fresh thyme
A handful of coarsely chopped parsley
Knob of butter
Sea salt and ground black pepper to taste

Heat the olive oil in the pan.
Add the chopped onion, garlic, chilli and bacon and gently fry until soften and golden.
Add the lentils, chopped carrots, celery, potato, bay leaves and thyme, just cover with water and bring to the boil.
Allow to simmer for 20 minutes and then add the smoked sausage. Add a little more hot water if it looks too dry. Continue to cook for another 10 minutes or until the vegetables and lentils are cooked.
Season to taste with sea salt and black pepper and finish by adding the butter, dried tomatoes and chopped parsley.
Serve with lightly steamed cabbage or courgettes or stir-fry them with a little olive oil and butter.

Sausage Meat and Bacon Wraps

You need the very best quality Lincolnshire style sausage meat to make this recipe. Plain pork sausages usually have less rusk or bread in them so if you do use standard sausage meat, add about 50gms of breadcrumbs or it will be a bit too rich. These delicious patties can be served with new potatoes and vegetables or like a burger in a bread bun with a salad on the side.

Serves 4. To scale up, just add extra sausage meat and bacon.
Equipment: a heavy, non-stick baking tray with low sides to allow browning.
Takes: 10 minutes to prep, 30 minutes to cook in the oven.

Ingredients
8 slices of streaky bacon

800g Lincolnshire sausage meat.
Freshly ground black pepper.

Pre-heat the oven to 200°C.
Divide the sausage meat into four equal sized balls and then shape them into a burger style patty.
Season generously with black pepper.
Wrap each patty around with 2 pieces of streaky bacon with the loose edges along the base.
Place them on a non-stick baking tray and bake/roast them for 30 minutes or until the bacon is crisp on the outside.

Variation
Smear a chicken breast with a little Dijon mustard, wrap with streaky bacon or Parma ham and cook as above. Delish!

Stews & Casseroles
Once you know the basics, you can make a delicious casserole with just about anything to hand and experiment with different flavour combinations.

Classic combinations
Chicken, white wine, cream and vegetables.
Pork with vegetables such as leeks, apples and cider, cream and mushrooms.
Lamb with red or white wine, carrots and pre-soaked beans.
Beef with red wine mushrooms and small whole onions or with beer, onions and carrots.

Properly slow cooking a casserole in the oven delivers the best flavour and the prep is reasonably quick, So, as the bulk of the cooking time takes care of itself, you can get on with other more important things while your casserole turns into something warm, comforting and tasty.

I prefer the rich finish that you get by cooking in a cast iron casserole in the oven, although most of the recipes could be prepped and put in a slow cooker if you have one. My mother used to swear by her pressure cooker but I always found it a bit terrifying and never learnt to use one! I always make double the quantity and freeze half, especially at the weekends, because it's not that much more trouble to prep. That way, I've always got a quick fuss-free supper ready for during the busy working week.

There aren't very many rules and techniques when it comes to making the perfect casserole.

First, prep the meat and vegetables. Then, heat up some oil and brown the meat you are using - just a few pieces at a time so that it browns rather than steams. Remove it from the pan and then sauté a mixture of 'the holy trinity' together (finely chopped carrot, onion and celery, maybe some garlic), cover with stock and/or wine, beer or cider, the meat and some fresh herbs, seasoning and pre-soaked pulses or vegetables. Cook slowly in the oven at about 150°C for at least a couple of hours (beef usually benefits from about 3 hours) and that way you'll make a brilliant, warming supper that's perfect every time.

Beef & Beer Stew with Fluffy Dumplings

Don't be concerned that the bitterness of the beer flavour will linger in this stew. It softens down into a really gorgeous sauce and totally hits the spot on a cold day. The dumplings should be well seasoned with white pepper and fluffy, but substantial. I don't usually serve mash as well, but if you're feeding a lot of people, that will make it go a bit further. Men love this stew. If the way to a man's heart really is through his stomach, this is the failsafe recipe!

Serves 6
Equipment: Large cast iron casserole dish
Takes: 15 minutes prep, 2 1/2 to 3 hours in the oven

Ingredients
1kg beef shin (the very best type of meat for a beef stew I think), try to get a piece of marrowbone too
1 heaped tablespoon of plain flour
1 clove of garlic, crushed
1 sprig of fresh thyme

2 fresh bay leaves
3 large onions, sliced
5 large carrots, peeled and chopped into large, bite-sized chunks
40g butter and a dash of olive oil
1 bottle of your favourite cooking beer – Belgian or English dark beer such as Bombardier
Salt and ground black pepper
Dumplings: *225g of plain flour, 1 level tablespoon of baking powder, ½ teaspoon of salt, 110g shredded suet, 150ml cold water, a dash of ground white pepper. Optional: 2 tablespoons of chopped fresh parsley*

Pre-heat the oven to 150°C.
Heat the oil and butter and brown the meat in batches. Set it aside on a plate.
Add the onions and cook them gently for five minutes.
Add the carrots, put the meat back in the pan.
Add the flour and stir it in.
Gradually stir in the beer and then the thyme.
Once it comes to a simmer, put the lid on and put it in the oven.
Leave it to cook for about 2½ hours – do not be tempted to open the lid and lose all the cooking steam!
To make the dumplings, mix the flour, baking powder, salt, pepper and suet in a large bowl. Add the water (and the parsley if you're using it) and mix it into a sticky dough. Add a little more water if they are too dry. Divide the mixture into roughly even sized portions (one dumpling per person) about a dessertspoon of the mixture into the casserole once it has cooked for 2 1/2 hours. Cover and continue to cook them in the steam for about 25 minutes. They will fluff up a lot.
Serve and enjoy the grateful groans of enjoyment.

Beef Bourguignon

This is a lovely old bistro classic and still totally dinner party worthy when made properly. The long cooking time also lends itself well to a weekend lunch so you can go to the pub or the park while it cooks away. The fragrance of beef, wine and herbs that will hit you when you walk back into your home will make you ravenously hungry! Delicious with creamed

potatoes to soak up all that tasty sauce.
Serves 6
Equipment: large oval oven proof casserole with a lid (preferably a cast iron Le Creuset) that can also be used on the hob
Time: 20 minutes prep, cooks for 3 hours in the oven. The meat marinates overnight before cooking.

Ingredients

1.5kg of well hung beef. A mixture of shin, shoulder and neck works beautifully. Cut it into bite-size chunks.
1 marrowbone (ask your butcher to cut you a piece small enough to go in your casserole dish – the marrow adds a lovely flavour to the stew and they don't usually charge for them either)
4 onions, roughly chopped
4 carrots, roughly chopped
3 cloves of garlic, finely chopped
4 sprigs of thyme
2 bay leaves
1 handful of roughly chopped parsley
1 bottle of red Burgundy
5 slices of chopped streaky bacon
Large knob of butter
1 large glass of brandy
150 ml Madeira
250 g mushrooms, sliced
200g of baby shallots, peeled and left whole
Salt and ground black pepper

Marinate the beef, onions, carrots, garlic and herbs in the wine overnight.
Heat the oven to 150°C.
Remove the meat and reserve the marinade.
Fry the bacon in the butter in the casserole and then add the meat to brown it. Do it in batches so it browns rather than steams!
Return all the meat to the pan and then add the brandy and flame it.
Add the Madeira.
Remove the vegetables from the marinade and then run it through a sieve. Discard the vegetables, pour the strained liquid over the meat and add the

marrowbone.

Bring it to a simmer, cover and then leave it to cook in the oven for 3 hours.

About ¾ of an hour before the end of the cooking time sauté the onions in some butter to caramelise them a little, season and then add to the stew. Heat another knob of butter in the same pan as the onions, and fry the sliced mushrooms until they are golden.

Add these to the stew about 5 minutes before you're ready to serve it. Adjust the seasoning and serve hot.

Gorgeous Goulash

This is a brilliant 'make ahead' stew and tastes even better if it's made and reheated the next day to allow the flavours to develop. I've come across a 'bitter sweet' Pimentón by Ramos at my local famer's market that completely transforms the flavour of this dish. You can buy a traditional one in a tin at most supermarkets these days. Ready ground spices can lose their strength very quickly if they don't get used fast enough. So, whatever you use, make sure it hasn't been in the cupboard for so long that it doesn't taste of anything but dust. Traditionally, this is served with freshly made noodles like spätzle but I've used buttered noodles like trofie - just as tasty and much easier. You could also serve it with plain boiled rice or potatoes.

Serves 4 to 6

Equipment: large oval oven proof casserole with a lid (preferably a cast iron Le Creuset) that can also be used on the hob

Time: 20 minutes prep, cooks for 3 hours in the oven

Ingredients

2 tablespoons of sunflower or olive oil
900g beef stewing steak, shin or skirt, cubed
1 1/2 tablespoosn Pimentón (smoked paprika)
1 tablespoon of sweet paprika
3 large onions, chopped
4 cloves of garlic, crushed
2 tablespoons of tomato paste
2 teaspoons of cider vinegar
1 teaspoon dark brown sugar

Jar of chopped roasted Pimentón peppers – optional but makes it more delicious
Sea salt and freshly milled black pepper
Two teaspoons of crushed caraway seeds
Enough water to cover
To serve: a 225ml carton of soured cream and a little paprika to sprinkle on top.

Pre-heat the oven to 160°C.
Heat the oil in the casserole on a high heat on the hob.
Brown the meat in small batches so it browns and seals rather than sweats. Put each batch to one side until they are all done.
Stir in the chopped onions and fry for a few minutes until brown, then add in the garlic.
Next add the tomato paste, , the caraway, the paprika, Pimentón, vinegar, sugar and water, season well and add the meat back in.
Let it come slowly up to a simmer and then put it in the oven for two to two and half hours. The sauce should be thickened, and the beef tender.
Add the peppers at the end to warm through.
Just before serving, let it stand for about five minutes and then marble the top with poured sour cream and sprinkled paprika.

Rich Oxtail or Ox Cheek Stew

There's quite a bit of effort involved with this dish but it's well worth it because the flavour is wonderful. My mother used to make a fantastic plain Oxtail stew and it's still one of our favourites although I make mine with wine or stout. There are three variations to this recipe: oxtail with red wine, oxtail with red wine and haricot beans or oxtail with stout. All are equally delicious, the ultimate comfort food. Cooked long and slowly in the oven, it is worth it for the aroma alone. It can also be cooked ahead of time and reheated. You can substitute ox cheek for oxtail with these recipes – it's inexpensive and easier if you can't be bothered to take the meat off the bones of an oxtail. I never serve it with the bones in because it's more difficult to serve it out evenly.

Serves 4
Equipment: large oval oven proof casserole with a lid (preferably a Le Creuset) that can also be used on the hob
Takes: 20 minutes prep, cooks for 3 hours or more in the oven

Ingredients

1 large oxtail, cut into pieces or two ox cheeks.
2 tablespoons sunflower oil
2 tablespoons of plain flour
1 teaspoon mustard powder
4 medium carrots, peeled and cut into large chunks
2 medium onions, sliced
2 cloves of garlic, crushed
1 medium swede, cut into medium sized chunks
3 large celery stalks, chopped
1 spring fresh thyme
2 bay leaves
425 ml hot beef stock
425 ml red wine or stout
Small bunch of fresh flat leaf parsley, finely chopped (half for cooking, half for serving)
Sea salt and freshly milled pepper
Optional: 225g haricot beans

If you are going to use the dried beans, pre-soak the beans in cold water overnight or bring to the boil and then leave to soak for 3 hours. Tinned ones don't really work as well but, if you do use them, only add them for the last hour of cooking or they will dissolve into mush.
Pre-heat the oven to 150°C.
Prepare the vegetables as above.
Put the flour and mustard powder into a plastic freezer or sandwich bag with a pinch of sea salt and ground black pepper. Place the oxtail pieces or ox cheeks in the bag and shake until each piece is coated thoroughly.
Heat the oil in the casserole on the hob.
Put the oxtail or ox cheek pieces in the oil and cook each side until nutty and brown. Remove and set aside.
Add some more oil and gently soften the vegetables until flecked with brown spots.
Stir in a little more flour and then add the hot stock gradually to avoid lumps.
If you are using dried beans, drain them and add to the casserole.
Add the oxtail or cheek, red wine or stout, thyme, parsley and bay leaves

and black pepper (no sea salt until the end of cooking if you are using the beans as it makes them tough).

Stir and bring to a simmer then place in the oven to cook slowly for at least three hours, the longer the better (check and stir half way through).

Go and do something else.

When it's ready, remove the oxtail pieces and remove the meat from the bone (if it is cooked thoroughly it will literally just fall off – it can be fiddly but is worth the effort). If using cheek, just shred the meat and remove any bits of skin that will spoil the finished dish. If there is too much fat floating on the surface of the casserole, just skim it off with a spoon.

Add the meat back into casserole and discard the bones, sprinkle with parsley before serving. Serve with a green vegetable like lightly cooked cabbage or courgettes if you cook the variation with beans, or with piles of creamy mash.

Suffolk Cider & Pork Loin Casserole

This is another recipe that I used to make to use up a glut of apples but it is just as nice made with cider alone so you can make it any time of the year. It's buttery, creamy and 'melt in the mouth' delicious.

Serves 4 – serve with rice or mash
Equipment: a frying pan and an ovenproof casserole.
Takes: 20 minutes prep, 60 minutes to cook

Ingredients
4 trimmed loin chops
1 large onion, finely sliced
1 clove of garlic, crushed
50g butter
4 springs of fresh thyme
250ml Aspalls's dry Suffolk cider
Salt and freshly ground black pepper
150ml double cream
Finely chopped parsley
Optional: 1 large Cox's dessert apple, peel left on, cored and thickly sliced

Pre-heat the oven to 180°C.

Melt half the putter in the frying pan.

Colour the pork chops until golden brown – it should take about 5 minutes, the rest of the cooking will be done in the oven. Put them into the ovenproof casserole.

Add the rest of the butter and fry the onion and garlic until soft (about 5 minutes).

Add a little more butter to cook the sliced apples if using so that they caramelise slightly. Place them over the pork.

Add the cider and the fresh thyme to the pan, bring it up to simmer and add the seasoning.

Add the cider to the casserole and cook it in the oven for about an hour and half or until the pork is cooked. The pork should be slightly flaky and melting.

Stir in the cream just before serving, check the seasoning and add the parsley. Remove the thyme stalks.

Cook the rice or mash about 10 minutes before you need it.

Variation: Cook with white wine rather than cider, exchange the apples for mushrooms and add a dessertspoon of mustard to the sauce.

Country Chicken Stew

This is a really tasty everyday chicken casserole dish; the carrots, celery and leeks in it complement the chicken perfectly. Serve with creamy mash and it's a 'hug on a plate' on a cold day.

Serves 4
Equipment: Large cast iron, lidded casserole dish
Takes: 25 minutes to prep, cooks in 2 hours.

Ingredients
12 skinned chicken thighs cut into bite sized pieces – much tastier and less expensive than breast meat
3 large carrots, 2 medium leeks, 2 large sticks of celery, 1 courgette – clean and prep the veg and cut in equal sized chunks on the angle – it just looks prettier!
The soft leaves from the celery, finely chopped
1 large onion
25g butter

1 tablespoon of plain flour
1 fat clove of garlic, crushed
Fresh parsley
A large glass of white wine (drink the rest with it!)
A chicken stock cube or a ½ litre of chicken stock

Pre-heat the oven to 150°C.
Gently brown the onions and then the chicken, vegetables and garlic in the butter.
Scatter over the flour and cook it through for a few minutes.
Add the wine and then the stock – stir gently and bring to a simmer.
Add the celery leaf and then leave it in the oven for a couple of hours until the vegetables and chicken are cooked through.
Just before serving stir in the chopped fresh parsley.

Burgundy Chicken

This is another French bistro classic and a lovely weekend supper or dinner party dish. It may not be fashionable in restaurants these days but it's one of our family favourites and always reminds us of bygone holidays. Buy the best quality chicken that you can, use a decent bottle of red Burgundy and don't be tempted to omit the brandy. The alcohol cooks off and gives a real depth of flavour that's a winner every time.

Serves 4
Equipment: Large cast iron lidded casserole dish
Takes: 25 minutes to prep, 2 hours to cook

Ingredients
1 whole chicken, jointed or 4 leg joints
150g thick streaky bacon cut into lardons
20 small shallots
2 whole cloves of garlic
65g butter
½ glass of brandy
1 bottle of red Burgundy
1 bay leaf and a couple of springs of thyme
Salt and pepper

1 dessertspoon of caster sugar
200g button mushrooms
Buerre manié - 1 tablespoon of flour mashed up with 60g of soft butter

Pre-heat the oven to 140°C.
Fry the chicken joints, bacons and shallots in half of the butter.
Once it is golden brown, add the brandy and flame it.
Add the red wine, herbs, garlic, salt and pepper.
Bring it to the boil, add the sugar, cover and put in the oven for about 2 hours until the chicken is cooked.
Remove the garlic and herbs.
Sauté the mushrooms in a small amount of butter and add to the sauce about 5 minutes before you want to serve.
To thicken the sauce, put the casserole on the hob and gradually stir in the buerre manié in little pieces. Keep stirring until the sauce has thickened and looks glossy.
Serve with creamy, buttery mash.

Slow Baked Lamb with Beans

This is a great dish for a lot of people on a cold day and is very, very easy to do. The lamb should be 'melt in the mouth' tender and the bed of beans and vegetables are served as a tasty and filling side dish. Tinned beans are not an acceptable substitute for this dish, so remember to put dried beans out to soak the night before you want them. Serve with green vegetables such as shredded cabbage and creamed potatoes.

Serves 6
Start on the hob, cook slowly in the oven for 4 hours at 170°C.or 8 hours at 140°C.
Equipment: Large roasting dish
Takes: 30 minutes prep, cooks in four hours. Pre-soak the beans the night before.

Ingredients
I large leg or a shoulder of lamb
500g dried beans such as cannellini or borlotti beans
4 large onions – chopped

4 cloves of garlic, peeled and crushed
2 carrots peeled and finely chopped
2 sticks of celery finely chopped
1 fresh bay leaf
3 large sprigs of fresh rosemary – washed and finely chopped.
250 ml dry white wine
1 tablespoon of olive oil
Sea salt and pepper
3 tablespoons of freshly chopped parsley

Put the beans into a large bowl of cold water and soak them overnight. The following day, drain them, put them in a saucepan of fresh water with the bay leaf and cook them according to the instructions on the packet – usually they need to be boiled and then simmered for anywhere between 20 minutes to an hour. Don't add any salt or they will be tough. Reserve the cooking water.

Preheat the oven to 170°C.

Chop the onions, carrot, and celery into small pieces – about the size of the nail on your little finger and crush the garlic.

Season the lamb generously with sea salt and ground black pepper.

Put the roasting tin on to the hob on a fairly high heat and then sear the lamb, fat side down, to give it colour and render some fat into the pan. Take the lamb out of the pan and set aside.

Add the oil to the pan and then the chopped vegetables to the pan and cook for about 5 minutes.

Add the cooked beans, the chopped rosemary, the wine and enough of the bean water to cover the mix and then bring it to the boil.

Place the lamb back in the roasting dish on top of the bean mixture, cover the tin with foil baggily but with the sides tightly sealed – it will cook in the steam.

Place it in the oven for a good 3 hours until the lamb is soft and well cooked. Take off the foil and cook uncovered for another half an hour or so. This will evaporate some of the liquid from the bean and vegetable mixture and brown the meat a little.

Remove from the oven, take the lamb out of the roasting dish and let rest for 10 minutes and then carve roughly on to a serving plate. It should really fall off the bone.

Check the bean and veg mixture, if it seems too watery, put it on the hob and simmer off the sauce until it has reduced and is quite thick. Check the seasoning and stir in the fresh parsley – serve it hot as a side dish.

Suffolk Lamb Hotpot

There are many, many different recipes for a traditional hotpot especially if you're from Lancashire. Well, I'm from Lincolnshire originally and have lived in Suffolk for 25 years so this is my version! Warming and fragrant with rosemary, this is autumn or winter bliss. Serve with pickled red cabbage on the side.

Serves 4

Equipment: large ovenproof dish – it needs to be about 5 cm deep and 27 cm square.

Takes: 30 minutes prep, cooks in the oven for about an hour and a half

Ingredients

7 medium sized potatoes, peeled and thinly sliced
30g butter
1 leek, sliced in 1 cm thick coins
4 carrots, peeled and cut on the diagonal
1 small swede, peeled and chopped into even bite sized chunks
1 parsnip – peeled and chopped
900g chopped shoulder of lamb
2 tablespoons of Worcestershire sauce
2 sprigs of fresh rosemary, finely chopped
2 tablespoons of seasoned flour
3 tablespoons of sunflower oil
1/2 litre of chicken stock

Preheat the oven to 150°C.

Toss the lamb in the seasoned flour and brown in batches in a frying pan of hot oil. Set the browned lamb to one side in the ovenproof dish.

Gently sauté the vegetables and the leftover flour in the pan for about 7 or 8 minutes until slightly softened.

Add the stock, the Worcestershire sauce and the rosemary. It should thicken up slightly.

Season to taste and pour over the meat.
Layer slices of potato over the top and dot with butter.
Cover with foil or a lid and cook in the oven for about and hour and half.
Turn up the heat to about 180°C, remove the foil so the potatoes can crisp and brown.
Serve hot with pickled red cabbage on the side.

Perfect English Sunday Roasts

A traditional English Sunday lunch means a meat roast with all the appropriate trimmings – a sauce, gravy, Yorkshire pudding, stuffing, roast and/or mashed potatoes, green vegetables and root vegetables. It's more than just a meal; a cold winter chill outside, the smell of roasting beef wafting in from the kitchen, an extra log on the cottage fire, a lazy read of the Sunday papers, a decent glass of wine or a pint of your favourite bitter…mmmm, heavenly. Done well, a proper roast is a thing of joy and what Sundays were made for.

Much like an English breakfast, successful roast lunches or dinners are all about timing. The prep is straightforward but getting it all ready and hot at the same time is what makes it tricky. To make it stress-free, just decide what time you want to sit down to eat and then work your timings backwards. Write them down and stick to them religiously.

Always make sure that you have enough oven space or hob rings for all the dishes you want to make. If you cook too many dishes without planning how you'll get them cooked at the same time, you'll be the one getting all hot and bothered, with half of your meal uncooked.

The traditional combinations

Roast beef, Yorkshire pudding, roast potatoes, horseradish sauce and mustard. A selection of whole roasted onions, roasted beetroot, sautéed greens, cauliflower cheese or parsnip gratin and braised carrots all make perfect accompaniments.

Roast pork, sage and onion or apple and chestnut stuffing, applesauce or whole roasted apples. Braised carrots, greens, roast and/or creamed potatoes work well.

Roast lamb and mint sauce with roast potatoes or gratin dauphinoise and a selection of braised vegetables are favourites.

Roast chicken, sage and onion stuffing, bread sauce, roast or creamed potatoes with a selection of steamed green and root vegetables.

Roast turkey (usually only at Christmas) is just a Sunday roast with knobs on – cranberry sauce, chestnut stuffing, bread sauce and plenty of slightly fancier side dishes such as glazed carrots, maple roasted parsnips, sprouts with bacon, glazed shallots and pancetta.

All roasts benefit from a seasonal selection of your favourite **vegetables** – contemporary mixes or traditional choices including peas, broad beans, French beans, courgettes, cabbage, broccoli, spinach, sprouts, carrots (always necessary for a balance of colour on the plate according to my Mother-in-law), beetroot, parsnips, mashed swede or creamed leeks.

For **dessert**, a fruit crumble or pie with lashings of custard make the experience complete!

Cooking tips

1. The number of people you'll be feeding and the weight of the joint will determine the cooking time.
2. Always buy your meat from a proper butcher. Supermarket meat is hardly ever up to much in terms of flavour because it simply hasn't had enough time to mature properly beforehand and it has all the fat cut off, particularly beef. Beef should be dark red with rich, creamy coloured fat not the colour of old bubble gum with white fat. Better to eat less meat than lots of poor quality stuff.
3. If you aren't sure how much to buy, just tell your butcher how many people you're cooking for and he will advise you. Leftover beef and pork is great for sandwiches or eaten cold the next day with a baked potato and salad.
4. A joint with a bone like a rib of beef or a leg of lamb will obviously weigh more, so make sure that you buy a piece with enough meat to bone ratio.
5. Pork and chicken should be thoroughly cooked in that the juices will run clear if you prick it with a sharp skewer, but not so overcooked that it is dry; lamb is best pink, beef is best just past rare.
6. Those misguided enough to prefer well-done beef can have the end pieces, save the middle and more rare slices for everyone else.
7. Meat must always be taken out of the fridge and be brought to room

temperature before cooking or the timings in the table won't work.
8. Once deemed cooked, all meat should be taken out of the oven put on a warmed plate or carving board, covered loosely with foil and rested for 20 minutes before serving. It will be easier to carve, more succulent and it won't taste chewy when you eat it. It will continue to cook a little which is why you really shouldn't overcook beef.
9. Cook all meats at the highest heat indicated for the first 20 minutes to develop browning on the outside (what Hugh Fearnly-Whittingstall calls 'the sizzle') and then cook the inside of the joint at the lower temperature outlined for the times in the table below.
10. Slice a few pieces of onion, carrot and celery to sit the meat on (and a few meat bones if the butcher gives them to you) so that you get a yummy, well-flavoured and caramelised stock to make your gravy with.
11. All ovens vary so these times are guidelines not the gospel – with practice you'll develop the knack of recognising when something is cooked properly in your own kitchen.

Roast pork

The skin must be completely dry, well scored with a sharp knife and cooked in a shallow roasting tray if you want good, crispy crackling.
Roast for 20 minutes at 210°C, then reduce the oven to 180°C and cook for 25 minutes per 500g for well done meat or 30 minutes per 500g for very well done. To test if it is cooked, run a skewer through it to test if the juices run clear (not pink) and pulls out easily. Leave it in and test at ten-minute intervals until it passes the clear test. Take it out when done, place on a warm plate, cover loosely with foil and rest for 20 minutes before carving.

Roast beef

Only cook large joints of beef, about 350kg per person or 2kg for 6 people. Gently dust with a mixture of plain flour and English mustard powder before cooking.
Roast for 20 minutes at 220°C, then turn down the oven to 160°C and cook for 10 minutes per 500g for rare beef, 15 for medium, 20 for well done. Take it out when cooked to your satisfaction, place on a warm plate, cover loosely with foil and rest for 20 minutes before carving.

Roast lamb

Spike the skin a knife and fill with garlic and rosemary slivers before roasting (pieces of anchovy are also excellent and won't impart a fishy taste) and season the skin with sea salt and pepper.

Roast for 20 minutes at 220°C, turn the temperature down to 160°C, then cook for 12 minutes per 500g for rare, 16 for medium, 20 for well done. Take it out when cooked to your satisfaction, place on a warm plate, cover loosely with foil and rest for 20 minutes before carving.

Roast chicken

Lightly oil the skin and dust with ground sea salt and pepper (or paprika or cinnamon if you want to add a flavour twist) before roasting. Alternatively, push softened butter mixed with herbs and/or a bit of chopped pancetta) under the skin of the breast, stuff the empty carcass with fresh herbs or a whole onion or lemon for extra flavour.

Cook at 210°C for 15 minutes and then turn the oven down to 160°C. Allow about another 40 minutes to an hour for a bird that weighs an average of 1.5kg. Once cooked take it out of the oven and give it 20 minutes resting time. To test if it is cooked properly stick the point of a sharp knife in the leg – if the juices run clear it's done, if it's still bloody cook it for another 15 to 20 minutes and repeat the test until it's done. Don't eat undercooked bird – that way a visit to the hospital lies!

Foolproof timing

Based on cooking a beef joint of 21/4kg for six people to eat at 2pm.

11.20 Make up mustard or horseradish sauce and keep it out of the fridge.

11.30 Take the beef joint out of the fridge.

11.50 Peel the potatoes.

12.00 Preheat the oven to 220°C and then put the potatoes in their water in a pan, bring the water up to boil and then add a pinch of salt; parboil for 7 minutes.

12.12 Drain the potatoes, allow the steam to evaporate and agitate them in the pan to rough up the edges. Dust lightly with a little plain flour or semolina (a Nigella top tip that really works) for extra crunchiness.

12.15 Put the roasting pan in the oven with a knob of dripping.

12.20 Put the beef in the oven to roast.

12.45 Turn the beef down to cook at 160°C.

12.45 Put the roasting pan with dripping or goose fat for the potatoes in the oven.
12.46 Make the Yorkshire pudding batter.
12.55 Put the potatoes into the hot fat in the oven.
1.00 Prep any other vegetables - carrots, cabbage etc. Set the table, warm plates and serving dishes
1.25 Put the kettle on so you have hot water ready for your vegetables.
1.30 Put in enough oil or dripping to cover the base of the Yorkshire pudding pan.
1.35 Take the beef out of the oven and put the Yorkshire pudding pan in, turning up the heat back up to 220°C as you do so. Allow the beef to stand, covering it loosely with foil to keep it warm.
1.45 When the Yorkshire pudding fat is really hot take it out, add the pudding batter and put it back in the oven. Make the gravy – whisk in some plain flour to the meat juices, heat it on the hob, add in hot stock and/or a dash of Madeira or red wine. Keep it warm on the hob if you have room.
1.46 Put the vegetables on to cook – this will depend on what they are obviously!
1.55 Drain the vegetables and carry in hot serving dishes to the dining area along with the beef to be carved at the table.
2.00 Take out the roast potatoes and Yorkshire pudding, set them on serving plates and take them straight to the table. If you've made a crumble or pie for dessert, whack it in the oven now so it's ready after you've eaten the main event.
2.05 Relax, eat and enjoy the happy faces, groans of enjoyment and compliments! Have a glass of wine. Cheers!

Yorkshire Pudding

The secret to a good Yorkshire pudding is that the fat must be smoking hot before you add the batter and to season it well with white pepper. I prefer to make this in a large (27cm) square ovenproof baking dish as it goes quite nicely from oven to table, although a metal tin is the traditional choice. This serves four to six people perfectly well.

Ingredients
2 eggs

150 ml semi-skimmed milk
110 ml water
150g plain flour, sifted
A large knob of beef dripping (the home grown variety with a little beef jelly in is superb!) or 2 tablespoons of cooking oil
A really generous pinch of ground white pepper (it adds a lovely flavour and doesn't spoil the look of the batter that coarsely ground black pepper can do) and a pinch of Maldon sea salt

Mix the eggs, milk, salt and pepper together in a large bowl with a whisk. Allow this mixture to stand for 15 minutes and then whisk in the flour making sure that there are no lumps in the batter.
Heat your oven to 220°C – it should already be fairly hot if you are cooking meat already.
Meanwhile put the fat into your baking dish and then into the very hot oven. Make sure that you put it on a shelf that will allow room for the pudding to rise without catching the roof of the oven.
Once you can see the fat shimmering, take the pan out of the oven and pour the batter in. If it doesn't sizzle, it isn't hot enough.
This should cook at 220°C for about 20 minutes. Don't open the oven door during cooking or will either not rise at all or deflate.
Take it out of the oven when risen, golden and crisp. Serve immediately.

Apple Sauce

Woe betide me if I forget to make apple sauce to go with roast pork! If there's lots left, it's lovely with yoghurt for breakfast.

Peel and core two Bramley cooking apples, place in a metal saucepan and add the juice of half a lemon to stop it browning. You can use dessert apples such as Coxes instead and use less sugar.
Cook gently on a medium heat on the hob for about 10 minutes until the apples turn fluffy. Turn off the heat and allow it to cool. Add sugar to taste. Some people add a knob of butter or sieve the sauce but it is perfectly nice without, especially if you're calorie counting. A teaspoon of finely grated fresh ginger is a pleasant alternative and usually removes the need for much sugar. Serve slightly warm with roast pork.

Mint Sauce

You can buy this in a supermarket, but it's so easy to make and so much nicer to eat, you might as well make your own. My neighbour has given me jars of apple jelly flavoured with mint that also works really nicely; the shop bought jelly is often far too sweet.

Mix two tablespoons of chopped fresh mint with 2 tablespoons of white wine vinegar (I find malt vinegar is too strong), 1 tablespoon of water and a pinch of sugar. Adding a very finely chopped spring onion or a little red onion can add a nice tang and extra texture for a change. Serve with roast lamb.

Horseradish Sauce

Roast beef without horseradish? Unthinkable!

Mix half a jar of shop bought creamed horseradish with a tablespoon of crème fraîche or sour cream for a light and delicious sauce to serve with beef. Serve at room temperature. If you're lucky enough to be able to get a root of fresh horseradish, peel it and grate it but be careful because it's potent stuff; it can make your eyes run worse than a bag full of raw onions mixed with chilli!

Bread Sauce

This is traditional with turkey at Christmas and works well any time of the year with roast chicken.

Ingredients

2 small onions, peeled and each stuck with 2 cloves
1 bay leaf
4 peppercorns
A blade of mace or ¼ teaspoon ground mace
800ml whole milk
150g fresh white breadcrumbs
30g butter
2 tablespoons of double cream
Fresh nutmeg
A pinch of sea salt

Add the onions, milk, mace, peppercorns, a pinch of sea salt and bay leaves into a milk pan. Bring it to the boil; remove it from the heat, cover and leave to infuse for at least an hour. Strain the milk, put it back on a medium heat and sprinkle in the breadcrumbs. Cook for about 15 minutes, it should be quite thick by now. Just before serving, warm the butter and cream in another pan, grate a good dusting of nutmeg into it and then stir into the bread sauce. Adjust the seasoning. Serve with roast chicken or turkey.

My Sage & Onion Stuffing Mixes

I don't ever actually stuff anything with these because I prefer to serve them on the side with roast chicken or pork in an ovenproof ceramic dish. That way it's easier to cook and serve and it's simple to add to sandwiches afterwards if there are leftovers. They are ridiculously easy to make and beat any shop bought mixes hands down.

Serves 4 to 6
Equipment: mixing bowl and an oven proof baking dish
Takes: 20 minutes to prep, 30 minutes to cook

Ingredients version 1
450g good quality sausage meat from a good butcher
1 knob of butter
6 fresh sage leaves
1 slice of stale bread, wholemeal preferably
Freshly ground black pepper
1 egg, beaten
1 onion, very finely chopped or grated
1 dessert spoon of apple sauce
Christmas option: mix in a jar of peeled, chopped, cooked chestnuts and/or a spoonful of smooth pâté

Add the bread and the sage to a food processor or hand held processor and reduce to fine crumbs.
Melt the butter in a small pan and cook the chopped onion on a low heat for 10 minutes until soft and golden – set aside to cool.
Mix the crumb and herb mixture, the sausage meat, onion, pepper and egg together in a large bowl.
Grease a small oven proof baking dish, add the stuffing mixture and bake in

a hot oven, 200°C for 30 minutes.
Serve with roast chicken or roast pork

Ingredients - version 2, the lighter option
3 large onions, finely chopped
75g goose fat or butter
500g fresh white breadcrumbs from a good quality cut loaf
Finely grated zest of a lemon
4 tablespoons of chopped fresh sage
3 tablespoons of chopped English (curly) parsley
1 large egg, beaten
Salt and pepper

Add the bread, sage and parsley to a food processor or hand held processor and reduce to fine crumbs.
Melt the butter or goose fat in a small pan and cook the chopped onion on a low heat for 10 minutes until soft and golden brown – set aside to cool.
Mix the crumb and herb mixture, the lemon zest, onion, pepper and egg together in a large bowl.
Grease a small oven proof baking dish, add the stuffing mixture and bake in a hot oven, 200°C for 30 minutes.
Serve with roast chicken, goose or roast pork.

Perfect Steak
A properly cooked, tasty steak with sautéed potatoes and a tomato or crisp green salad is hard to beat and the work of moments. I'm always disappointed by steak ordered in a restaurant and besides, I'd rather them make me something I can't be bothered to cook at home, or with ingredients that are harder to buy than beef!

If you're serving it with a tomato salad, make it before you cook the steak.
If you're serving it with buttered spinach, cook it while the steak is resting.
If you're serving it with chips, make them while the steak is resting.
A baked potato should have gone into the oven a good hour before you serve the steak.
Buy your favourite cut of steak (ribeye or rump is generally the best flavour), and take it out the fridge at least 30 minutes before cooking. Cold meat straight of the fridge will lack flavour and will probably be cold in the

middle when you serve it.

Get a non-stick frying pan or griddle pan smoking hot. Lightly oil and then cook the steak for just 3 or 4 minutes on each side – it should be caramelised on the outside and medium rare on the inside. Finger test it to test its progress. If it feels soft and springy like the fleshy part of your palm just under your thumb, it's cooked. If it starts to feel hard, it's well done. A well-done steak is just a waste of good meat. Add a knob of butter to the pan and baste the steak quickly with it.

Take it off the griddle and place it on a warm plate or on a wooden board. Season with a little salt and black pepper. Cover and allow it to rest for 10 minutes and then serve. Don't ever be tempted to eat it straight after you've taken it out of the pan, the fibres need to rest and a rested steak will be juicier, more tender and easier to cut into.

Chubby Chops

Lamb or pork chops make a great quick supper at anytime of the year with a baked potato, side salad or lightly cooked vegetables on the side. Don't be tempted to cut the 'chubby' fat off before you cook them or they will lose flavour – by all means snip the outer rind in a few places to prevent it curling up the meat.

Pork Chops

These are best gently pan-fried with a knob of butter so that it's caramelised on the outside and creamy and moist on the inside, or oven roasted in a shallow roasting dish for about 30 to 40 minutes. My mother used to cook them slowly in the Aga – delicious! Pork must never be served rare by the way. Pork chops work beautifully sprinkled with chopped fresh sage, before cooking.

Lamb Chops

These are best grilled or lightly pan-fried in olive oil so they are still pink inside. Cooking time will vary with thickness, 30 minutes is about right for thick pork chops, but you only need about 10 minutes for lamb as a rule. Lamb chops work well marinated or rolled in olive oil, chopped rosemary and garlic and a drizzle of lemon juice. Serve with redcurrant, apple or mint jelly.

Chicken Marinato
Chicken breast or thigh pieces marinated and then cooked under the grill or in a hot pan on the hob for about 20 minutes in some oil or butter or straight on to a hot griddle make a fast and tasty lunch or supper dish.
I often make up a large batch of different 'marinatos' or marinades and add 2 or 4 pieces of chicken to a sealable freezer bag. That way, I can make one meal now and freeze the rest for another time.

My five favourite marinades
Just mix, add the chicken cook now, or freeze for later. Most are tasty either hot or cold.
1. The finely grated rind and juice of a lemon, crushed garlic, a tablespoon of olive oil, salt and pepper.
2. The finely grated rind and juice of a lemon, a tablespoon of olive oil, salt and pepper and chopped tarragon.
3. A tablespoon of olive oil, salt and pepper, a teaspoon of smoked Pimentón and a teaspoon of tomato paste.
4. A tablespoon of sunflower oil, salt and pepper, 2 teaspoons of my Madras curry powder, a dessertspoon of thick Greek yoghurt.
5. A tablespoon of sunflower oil, salt and pepper, 2 teaspoons of my Thai green curry paste, a dessertspoon of creamed coconut.

Boiled or Baked Ham
Baked ham always reminds me of my Grandma because that's what we always ate when she came to lunch on Thursdays. She also left us pocket money – happy days!

A home cooked ham is both delicious and simple to make; buy a decent sized joint as any leftovers and the stock have a multitude of tasty uses – risotto, omelette filling, pasta sauce or chopped up and added to a hearty soup, cauliflower or macaroni cheese.

Serve this version with new potatoes, carrots, cabbage and my mustard and parsley sauce.

Firstly, you need to get rid of the curing salt. The best thing is to either soak it in cold water overnight, or put the joint in a pot of cold water, bring it to the boil and then drain and throw the water away.
To cook, cover the joint with cold water and bring to the boil again with a carrot, a quartered onion, a stick of celery, a few chilli flakes and simmer for 20 minutes per pound. Nigella swears by cooking this in a bottle of, preferably cherry, coke, but I prefer my version having tasted both. When cooked, set aside and leave to rest and cool before carving.

You could also make a **baked gammon** by following step one, and then wrapping the joint in two large pieces of baking foil that you fold and seal around the edges to seal and create a kind of foil pillow to bake it in. Bake it in the oven for 30 minutes per 450g. Half an hour before the end, take the joint out, unwrap it, pour off and save the stock to use later. Cut away the top layer of rind, score the fat in a diamond pattern, smear it thickly with English mustard and sprinkle with Demerara sugar – bake it for another 30 minutes until golden. Remove from the oven, leave to cool and rest before carving.

To make **honey roast ham**, simply mix some runny honey and made English mustard or redcurrant jelly together, rub the joint with the mix and place it on a foil covered roasting dish in a very hot oven for about 20 to 25 minutes. Leave to cool and rest, and then carve to serve.

Sometimes, I discard the stock vegetables and whilst the meat is cooling I cook a few whole carrots, potatoes and a quartered cabbage to serve with it in the stock for extra flavour.

Keep the stock for making my mustard and parsley sauce, or put it in the freezer for a tasty risotto or as a base for a pea and ham soup on another day.

Mustard & Parsley Sauce

This is such a lovely accompaniment to cooked ham. Melt a generous knob of butter in a non-stick pan. Whisk in a couple of tablespoons of plain flour

(50g) to make a roux. Cook gently for a few minutes and then gradually and carefully ladle in the hot gammon stock until you have a smooth thick sauce. Add a dessertspoon of Dijon mustard and some finely chopped fresh parsley. Adjust the seasoning if necessary. Serve with the gammon and extra vegetables. Heaven!

A more traditional way to serve it is with a white sauce made with a roux of butter and plain flour as above, or butter and cornflour, and about 500ml of milk depending on how thick you want it. Add lots of freshly and finely chopped curly parsley to it. Lighten it with a little cream if necessary.

Pot Roasted Beef

Cheaper cuts of beef such as brisket and topside aren't really suitable for roasting but are delicious slowly braised in the oven. As with many of my recipes, I have a couple of variations just to ring the changes. Sometimes I just make this on a bed of sliced and seasoned onions and then liquidise the onions and the juices for the best ever tasting gravy. Sometimes I make it with wine and herbs or a tin of tomatoes.

Serves 6
Equipment: Large oval cast iron lidded casserole
Takes: 20 minutes prep, 2.5 hours cooking time

Ingredients
1.5kg beef brisket or topside
5 tablespoons olive oil
3 large carrots, finely chopped
2 onions, finely chopped
4 celery sticks, finely chopped
3 sprigs of rosemary
3 garlic cloves, finely chopped
1 bottle of red wine
Sea salt and pepper
Option: add a 400g tin of chopped tinned tomatoes

Pre-heat the oven to 140°C
Rub the beef with salt and pepper, heat the oil in a large pan, seal the joint

and remove.

In the same pan, add in the chopped vegetables, garlic and herbs and sweat them for a couple of minutes.

Put the meat back in the pan, and add the wine and bring to a simmer.

Put the lid on the casserole and put in the oven.

It should be cooked in about 2 and a half hours but check at 2 to see how it's progressing. To test the meat, gently stick it with a skewer to see if the juices run clear and if it comes out easily.

Remove the meat when it's cooked, allow it to rest for 10 minutes and then carve into slices. Serve with the vegetables and sauce. I like to add some chopped fresh parsley to the vegetables and some chopped raw tomato. Fantastic with mashed potato or, if you made the tomato based option, some buttered noodles.

'Empty Nesters' Liver Recipes

Nina has never shared my love of offal but these are my favourite recipes for cooking liver when the nest is empty! Maybe one day she'll see the light, I've included them anyway.

Pig's Liver with Bacon, Onions and Mustard

I only have to think about this dish and the lovely gravy it makes and my mouth starts watering, mmmm…...

Serves 4 – lovely with buttery mash
Equipment: Large cast iron lidded casserole, small frying pan.
Takes: 45 minutes

Ingredients

Enough pig's liver for four people cut into 4 or 8 strips/pieces
8 strips of streaky bacon
Clove of garlic – crushed
1 large onion – peeled and thinly sliced
Large knob of butter
2 tablespoons of Dijon mustard
A tablespoon of finely chopped parsley
Freshly ground black pepper

Preheat the oven to 150°C.
Gently sauté the onions and garlic in the butter in a frying pan on the hob.
Lay four of the bacon strips on the base of the casserole so that the liver can be placed on top of it.
Smear the mustard all over the liver and then scatter the onion mixture, the ground pepper and chopped parsley over it.
Layer the remaining 4 slices of bacon over the top to make a kind of liver and onion bacon sandwich.
Cover with the casserole lid and leave it cook in the oven for 30 minutes. The bacon, liver, mustard and onion mixture will make its own delicious gravy. You can also deglaze the pan with a tablespoon of wine vinegar if you would prefer a slightly sharper flavour.
Serve with buttery mash and your favourite green vegetable.

Calf's Liver
Another tasty winner, and so quick and easy to make.

Serves 4 – excellent with steamed new potatoes
Equipment: frying pan
Takes: 20 minutes

Ingredients
Enough calf's liver for 4 people cut into thin slices
3 thin rashers of streaky bacon
25g butter
A squeeze of lemon juice
A dessertspoon of finely chopped parsley

Fry the liver in hot butter on both sides quickly over a high heat.
Drain it and keep it hot on the serving dish.
Fry the bacon slices until crisp and use to garnish the finished dish.
Sprinkle with a squeeze of lemon and the chopped parsley.
Serve with the steamed new potatoes.

Lamb's Liver with Garlic
Excellent with the first Jersey Royals and some buttered spinach.

Serves 4
Equipment: frying pan
Takes: 20 minutes

Ingredients
Enough lamb's liver for 4 people cut into thin slices
4 cloves of finely chopped garlic
25g butter
Salt & pepper
4 tablespoons of sherry vinegar
A dessertspoon of finely chopped parsley

Over a high heat, fry the liver in hot butter quickly on both sides.
Season with salt and pepper and keep it hot on the serving dish.
Put the garlic in the frying pan and stir quickly so it doesn't go brown.
Immediately deglaze the pan with the wine vinegar and allow it to reduce by half.
Coat the liver with the sauce, sprinkle with the chopped parsley and serve immediately.
Serve with the steamed new potatoes or wilted spinach.

'The Famous Pork'

This is a Rick Stein menu that Stickman discovered and then made his party piece several years ago. It's an oriental spiced roast belly of pork with crackling to die for, served with plain rice, steamed pak choi and an oyster sauce based gravy. Everyone who eats it absolutely loves it. Everyone who tries it wants the recipe. People invite themselves to dinner and they either hope that this is what we'll be serving, or just request it outright. It would feature on any number of 'last supper' lists. Sublime doesn't even cover it. It can look a bit complicated to make at first glance, but you'll be surprised at how easy it is once you've made it the first time.

Serves: 6 to 8
Equipment: A large oven-roasting tray with a grill tray. The one that comes with your oven will be perfect so that it can slide in on the oven rails. A spice grinder/mortar and pestle. Steamer for the vegetables, pan for the rice.

Takes: 30 minutes to prep, 2 1/2 hours to cook. The pork must be spiced for a good 8 hours or more so remember to factor that into your planning. We usually do this the night before we make it.

Ingredients
1.5kg piece of thick belly pork with the bones removed and the rind intact – let the butcher take the bones out but don't let him score the rind.
1 tablespoon of Sichuan peppercorns
1 teaspoon of black peppercorns
2 tablespoons of Maldon sea salt flakes
2 teaspoons of Chinese five-spice powder
2 teaspoons of Golden caster sugar
Enough basmati rice for however many people you are feeding. Soak it in a bowl of cold water about an hour and then drain it before you want to cook it.
Enough pak choi for however many people you are feeding – allow at least one medium sized head of pak choi per person. Sugar snap peas work well as an extra vegetable.

Chinese Sauce/Gravy
4 teaspoon of sunflower oil
2 teaspoons of sesame oil
8 tablespoons of oyster sauce
2 tablespoons of dark soy sauce

Mix the ingredients in a small pan, just heat through before pouring over the steamed greens.

With a fine skewer, prick the skin of the pork all over. Go through the fat but don't go so deep that you pierce the flesh.

Lay the pork on a rack over the sink. Boil a kettle of water and pour it all over the skin. Let it drain and then dry it off well with some kitchen towel. Heat a heavy based frying pan over a dry heat. Add the Sichuan and black peppercorns and swirl them around for a bit until they darken a little and give off an aromatic scent.

Transfer the peppercorns to a spice grinder and grind them into a fine powder. Tip them into a bowl with the salt, sugar and five-spice powder. Turn the pork flesh side up on a large plate or tray and then rub the spice mix into the flesh. Set aside for at least 8 hours somewhere cool. We just put ours in the fridge. You may want to cover it with Clingfilm to stop the fragrance of the spices tainting anything else in the fridge.

When you're ready, preheat the oven to 200°C.

Turn the pork skin-side up and place it on a rack resting on top of a roasting tin (or the oven grill pan). Fill it with water to make a bain-marie. Roast the pork on this high heat for 15 minutes, then lower the temperature to 180°C. Roast it for another 2 hours. Top up the water if it looks like it's going to dry out. This method ensures that the skin will crisp and crackle, and the meat will be mouth-wateringly tender and full of flavour.

After 2 hours, increase the oven temperature to 230°C and continue to roast the pork for another 15 minutes.

Remove from the oven and leave it cool for about 15 minutes. It should be served warm.

With a heavy bladed knife, cut the pork into bite-sized pieces and arrange them on a warmed serving platter.

Whilst the meat is cooling, cook the rice and lightly steam the greens. Dress the greens with the oyster sauce mix.

Serve the pork, rice and sauce dressed greens and wait for the groans of delight..

Thai Prawn Curry

This is a fast and delicious supper without resorting to the take-out menu, or useful if there's no branch of Wagamama in your neighbourhood and you want a decent Thai dish in your repertoire. I make this with prawns but you could also make it with thin strips of chicken.

Serves 4
Equipment: a wok and a saucepan for the rice
Takes: 25 minutes to prep, 10 minutes to cook

Ingredients
1 tablespoon of groundnut oil
400ml tin of coconut milk
2 packets of pak choi, bases quartered, leaves roughly chopped
A small pack of mangetout
320g raw king prawns
1 tablespoon of fish sauce
The juice of a lime
A handful of fresh basil leaves.
Basmati or Jasmine rice for 4 people
Green Thai curry paste (I usually have some in the freezer as I always make double) - 5 fat lemongrass stalks, chopped, 2 medium-hot green chillies, 25g peeled fresh ginger, 3 fat

garlic cloves, 50g chopped shallots, ½ teaspoon of sea salt, 1 teaspoon of shrimp paste.

Put the rice on to cook.
Put all the paste ingredients in a mini food processor with 3 tablespoons of water and blitz it to a smooth paste.
Heat the oil in the wok and add the paste.
Add the coconut milk and fish sauce.
Throw in the mangetout or baby corn and the pak choi until it wilts.
Add in the raw prawns – when they turn that lovely coral pink, they're cooked.
Add in the lime juice and the basil.
Serve over the rice in individual bowls.

Beef in Black Bean Sauce

If I ever do go to a Chinese restaurant, or order takeout, this is what I always have. I think my homemade version is equally good, if not better.

Serves 2
Equipment: a wok and a saucepan for the rice
Takes: 25 minutes to prep, 10 minutes to cook

Ingredients
300g sirloin steak, thinly sliced
1 tablespoon of groundnut oil
1 teaspoon of sesame oil
1 dessertspoon of dry sherry or rice wine
1 tablespoon of dark soy sauce
1 clove of garlic, crushed to a paste
1 green pepper, cored and cut in medium sized rough chunks
3 sticks of celery, de-strung and cut on the bias in similar sized pieces to the pepper
5cm piece of fresh ginger, peeled and finely grated
1 fresh green chilli, deseeded and finely chopped
½ an onion and cut in medium sized rough chunks
Half a jar of ready-made black bean sauce. I like the Who Hup brands.
Rice or noodles to serve

Put the rice or noodles on to cook.
Heat the oil in the wok until it's very hot.

Add the garlic, soy, ginger and chilli.
Add the beef and cook quickly.
Add the vegetables and cook quickly so that they don't lose their bite.
Add the black bean sauce.
Stir for another few minutes as it really cooks very quickly.
Serve with rice or noodles in warm dishes.

Aromatic Meat Curry

You can use literally any meat – chicken, lamb, beef - with this and it will taste fantastic. This can be made ahead of time and reheated and the flavour will improve. It's our absolute favourite curry dish.

Serves 4
Equipment: Spice grinder, mini-blender, cast iron casserole dish.
Takes: 30 minutes prep and an hour and a half to cook.

Ingredients
800g of meat - beef, lamb fillet, lamb shanks (4), chicken thigh meat or pork
2 tablespoons of sunflower oil
2 cloves of garlic, peeled
2cm piece of fresh root ginger, peeled
1 fresh green chilli
1 onion, peeled and finely sliced
4 cardamom pods
2 bay leaves
1 400g tin of chopped tomatoes
200ml beef or chicken stock
2 teaspoons of tamarind juice
Salt and freshly ground black pepper
2 banana shallots, finely sliced
Aromatic curry powder (I usually have a quantity ready made) - 2 tablespoons of coriander seeds, 2 tablespoons of fenugreek seeds, 1 tablespoon of mustard seeds, 1 teaspoon of cumin seeds, ½ teaspoon fennel seeds, 1 teaspoon black peppercorns, 1 cinnamon stick, broken into pieces, 3 cloves, 1 tablespoon of ground turmeric
Nan breads, chapatis or rice to serve and a cucumber raita

Make the curry powder in the spice grinder.
Blend the ginger, garlic and chilli with a tablespoon of water to a paste.

Heat the oil in the casserole dish.
Brown the meat in batches and put to one side.
Add a little more oil to the pan, add the onions and cook for a few minutes.
Add the cardamom and bay leaves.
Add 2 ½ tablespoons of the Madras powder, stir it in and then add the paste.
Add the stock, tomatoes and tamarind juice, stir and bring to a simmer.
Return the meat to the sauce and cook in the oven for up to an hour and a half.
Check the seasoning before serving.
Fry the sliced shallots until crispy to garnish the curry.
Serve with breads, rice and cucumber or mint raita.

CHAPTER FOUR: RICE, GRAINS & PULSES

"Not all of us were working at the same time, but enough of us... Hank Fonda knew how to cook rice. We lived pretty much on a rice diet."

James (Jimmy) Stewart
(Hollywood Screen Legend)

Depending on which Western diet fad is currently in ascendance, rice, bread, pasta and so on can be food heroes or villains. Let's not forget, that in many parts of the world where meat is not a central part of the diet for reasons of religion, availability or affordability, grains and pulses are the stuff of life and are prepared in many delicious and nutritious ways!

Perfect Basmati Rice

Apart from when I'm making a pudding or a risotto, I always use basmati rice – the Rolls Royce of rice. It's a bit more expensive than long grain, but I simply prefer the nutty flavour and it always turns out perfectly. I usually cook way more rice than I need, especially if I have visitors – it just looks mean if there's not enough. I love to eat the leftovers cold with a few shakes of light soy sauce. Measure about 65ml per person out in a jug and add another portion or two for the pot if in doubt.

There a few golden rules to perfect rice every time…

I pre-soak it in cold water for about an hour and then drain it before cooking.

Use a wide, flat-bottomed frying pan with a lid to cook it. My battered old pan is more than 20 years old, but it never lets me down. It's a shallow pan and the rice can spread out over a wide surface area, and the lid is so tight that it allows the rice to cook in the trapped steam.

I always add a tiny bit of sunflower oil to the hot pan and coat the rice grains before adding boiling water and a couple of good pinches of sea salt. Just cover the rice with water so there's about ½ a centimetre of water above the line of rice.

Bring it to the boil, put the lid on tightly, turn off the heat and then just leave it for 10 minutes undisturbed. Don't be tempted to peek, or the steam will escape. Don't stir it until it's cooked, otherwise it will turn starchy and sticky.

Once it's ready, take of the lid, put a clean tea towel over it and lightly fork through it to fluff it up before serving in a warmed dish.

For extra flavor, you can fry a few onions in the pan before you add the rice, or some aromatic spices such as cardamom pods, a couple of whole cloves, a bay leaf, some cinnamon bark, a little saffron soaked in milk to make a pilau. A light chicken stock to make a pilaf is also a tasty alternative.

Couscous and Bulgur Wheat

Quick, tasty, cheap and versatile these dishes can be made with either grain and can be served hot with a tasty lamb stew, or cold as the basis for a salad.

Serves 4
Equipment: medium sized lidded saucepan
Takes: 5 minutes to prep, 15 to 20 minutes to cook

Ingredients

255g couscous
1 medium shallot, finely chopped
1 tablespoon of olive oil
A pinch of red chilli flakes
A teaspoon of fennel seeds
A teaspoon of cumin seeds
425ml hot chicken or vegetable stock or 425ml hot water and a teaspoon of salt

Heat the oil and soften the chopped shallot.
Add in the spices and the stock.
Stir and bring to the boil and then turn off the heat.
Leave it to sit for up to 2 minutes and it will cook in the steam.
Lightly fork to fluff it up and serve in warmed dish.

Variations

Add a tin of chickpeas to make it more substantial.
Let it go cold and add half a deseeded and chopped cucumber and a

tablespoon of chopped flat parsley and fresh mint leaves, stir it through with a dressing of olive oil and the finely grated rind and juice of a lemon. Season to taste.

Kasha
Cook Bulgur wheat according to the instructions on the packet but with hot chicken stock instead of plain water and add a handful of broken up vermicelli noodles. Serve hot or cold. Perfect with roast lamb.

Pepper Salad
Cook Bulgur wheat with plain water according to the instructions on the packet. Let it go cold and add halved cherry tomatoes and roasted chopped red peppers. Stir it through with a dressing of olive oil and the grated rind and juice of a lemon (or salted lemon rind). Season to taste.

Tabbouleh
Using just the bulgur wheat and no seasonings but salt, let it go cold and add half a deseeded and chopped cucumber and a handful of chopped cherry tomatoes, 2 tablespoons of chopped flat parsley and fresh mint leaves. Stir it through with a dressing of olive oil, the juice of a lemon and a pinch of allspice. Season with salt and black pepper to taste.

Risottos
The secret to a great risotto (apart from the 20 odd minutes of patience it takes to stir it) is the stock, and using good quality rice such as Arborio or Carnaroli. If you don't have any of those, make something else for supper. If you do, you'll be rewarded with a delicious treat. It's pretty high on calories though so limit how often you eat it if you are watching your weight.

Pea & Ham Risotto
Quite possibly, my favourite of all risottos. I like a squeeze of lemon on mine at the end to cut the richness.

Serves 4 to 6
Equipment: a large wide base frying/sauté pan for the risotto, a saucepan for heating the stock
Takes: 10 minutes prep, 2 minutes stirring

Ingredients

400g risotto rice
1 litre of ham stock
400g chopped cooked ham
50g frozen petits pois
1 tablespoon of olive oil
70g butter
3 finely chopped shallots
2 cloves of garlic, crushed to a paste
2 sticks of celery, de-strung and finely chopped
100ml Noilly Prat for preference or dry white wine
Maldon sea salt and pepper
80g grated Parmesan

Heat the stock, but don't let it boil
Heat the oil in the sauté pan and sweat the shallots and celery for a few minutes until they are translucent and soft, and then the garlic paste.
On a medium heat, add the rice and coat it with the oil for 2 to 3 minutes. Add the vermouth, and keep stirring to cook off the alcohol and leave the flavour.
Add the first ladle of stock and keep stirring. As each ladle is absorbed, add another and then another. Taste for seasoning – you won't need to add much salt if the ham stock is salty.
Keep stirring, and the heat at medium. The liquid must be absorbed slowly or the outside will be soft and the inside will be too hard. A little bite is what you're aiming for but not a crunch. Keep adding stock until it's gone. The risotto should be slightly liquid not dry.
When it tastes ready stir in the ham and peas to warm through, take it off the heat, stir in the Parmesan and the butter.
Serve immediately on warmed plates. Dress with a little olive oil.

Pancetta and Rosemary Risotto

Use exactly the same method but use chicken stock, fry 60g of chopped pancetta in at the vegetable stage and then add a couple of tablespoons of finely chopped fresh rosemary leaves.

Mushroom Risotto

Use the same method as above, but use chicken stock instead. Sauté 250g of mixed mushrooms (wild and cultivated) in some butter and stir into the risotto once you've stirred in a few ladles of stock. Finish with some finely chopped parsley and, for a real treat, drizzle with truffle oil. Heavenly, especially in autumn if you've foraged for fresh wild mushrooms (ones that you know won't poison you obviously!).

Pea & Prawn Risotto

Use exactly the same method, but substitute the ham stock with a light chicken or fish stock, omit the Parmesan and butter and stir in 300g of cooked prawns and 200g of petits pois. Garnish with chopped fresh mint.

Puy Lentils

I love these nutty flavoured little blue-green 'caviar' lentils. They're great served with sausages or chops. These are my two favourite recipes.

Puy Lentils with Wine, Rosemary & Sage

Serves 4
Equipment: saucepan for boiling the lentils, frying pan
Takes: 30 minutes

Ingredients

225g Puy lentils
300ml beef stock
3 tablespoons of olive oil
300ml of red wine, boiled rapidly down until reduced to 3 tablespoons
2 garlic cloves crushed into a paste
2 finely chopped shallots
1 red chilli, seeded and chopped
2 sprigs of rosemary – leaves finely chopped
3 fresh sage leaves, finely chopped
2 tablespoons of flat-leaf parsley, chopped
Salt and ground black pepper

6 sun blush tomatoes, chopped into pieces

Cook the lentils in boiling salted water for 15 minutes. Drain.
Heat the olive oil in the frying pan; add the shallots and cook for a few minutes, then add the garlic paste, sage, rosemary and chilli.
Add the lentils, beef stock and red wine reduction. Simmer until the liquid has reduced, and the lentils are completely cooked.
Add in the sun blush tomatoes and season to taste.
Stir in the parsley and serve in a warmed dish.

Puy Lentils with Spinach

Serves 4
Equipment: saucepan for boiling the lentils, frying pan
Takes: 30 minutes

Ingredients

225g Puy lentils
300ml beef stock
3 tablespoons of olive oil
2 garlic cloves crushed into a paste
2 finely chopped shallots
250g spinach, washed
Salt and ground black pepper

Heat the olive oil in the frying pan. Add the shallots and cook for a few minutes, then add the garlic paste.
Add the lentils and beef stock. Simmer until the liquid has reduced and the lentils are completely cooked.
Chop the spinach finely and add to the lentils so that it wilts and clings to them.
Season and serve in a warmed dish.

WHAT'S4TEAMUM?

CHAPTER FIVE: VEGETABLES

"After all the trouble you go to, you get about as much actual "food" out of eating an artichoke as you would from licking 30 or 40 postage stamps".
Miss Piggy
(Leading Lady – The Muppet Show)

Unlike Her Pigginess, I love vegetables of every kind and, treated with respect, they almost never taste of stamps.

Vegetable top tips

Fresh is best
The fresher vegetables are, the better they will taste. Buy in season and as locally as possible. The further they travel, the earlier they are picked, the less flavour and nutritional value they will have. There's a table of what's in season and when at the end of the book. However, frozen vegetables like peas, broad beans, soy (edamame) beans and sweet corn can prove the exception and are far better taste-wise than tinned vegetables. If you grow your own vegetables, freeze any gluts or make chutneys and sauces to use at another time.

Keep it simple - the more simply vegetables are cooked and prepared, the better they usually taste.

Steam. If you have a steamer, steam vegetables such as baby asparagus, carrots, parsnips, swede, broccoli and courgettes so as to preserve the nutrients and their colour. Vitamin C is water-soluble, so if you boil vegetables and don't use the liquid for gravy, sauce or soup, you throw away much of the goodness.

Wilt. Vegetables such as cabbage or spinach are good stir-fried, or wilted quickly in only the water that still clings to them after washing.

Dressing. Eat vegetables plain, or dress them in a little butter and freshly grated nutmeg (carrots, parsnips, spinach), or drizzle with a tasty olive oil and a little sea salt (broccoli, cabbage, leeks, spinach).

Wash. Salad leaves and vegetables should always be washed in clean water before cooking (bagged supermarket vegetables have often been washed in chlorine). Use a salad spinner for salad leaves so that your vinaigrette or other dressing will coat them properly. A salad spinner is a cheap kitchen gadget and fun to use. Kids love to help with that part. Dry vegetables with a tea towel or kitchen paper after washing if you are going to cook them in oil so as to prevent them from spitting and burning you.

Peel smart. Use a decent vegetable peeler so that you don't waste or peel off too much, as most of the nutrients lie directly beneath the skin. Only peel vegetables if you have to; new carrots simply need to be scrubbed, courgettes do not need to be peeled at all, onions always need peeling and so do old potatoes (unless being baked) but not new ones.

Cooking from frozen. Vegetables such as peas and sweetcorn usually just need to be brought to the boil, left for a minute and then drained quickly so as not to spoil their delicate and fresh flavour.

Salting. Some recipes will tell you to salt and drain aubergines or courgettes before cooking to remove bitterness. The varieties we use in this country don't really require this – I never bother unless I'm salting to remove extra moisture.

Timing. Whatever you do, don't overcook vegetables. Some vegetables can be cooked in a couple of minutes otherwise they go hard or soggy. For example peas, shredded cabbage and dwarf beans need to be put in boiling water and more or less just heated through. Root vegetables such as carrots and potatoes need slightly longer, about 10 to 15 minutes. Brassicas such as broccoli and cauliflower should always be steamed, usually for no more than about 8 minutes.

Test. To tell if vegetables such as potatoes are cooked, simply prick them with the point of a sharp knife. If it gives, they're cooked, if it doesn't they're not!

Preparation. Cut vegetables such as potatoes into evenly sized pieces. That way they will cook evenly and avoid lumping when being mashed.

Roast. Most vegetables roast very well – potatoes, squashes, aubergines, peppers, beetroot, celeriac, garlic, onions, tomatoes and fennel are all delicious. Combine aubergine, peppers, courgettes and onions in summer, and combinations of root veg such as carrot, parsnip and swede in winter.

Stir-fry. Cabbage, courgettes, beans, sprouts, celery, pak choi, leeks, spinach, spring onions and peas all sauté or stir fry in oil or butter very well.

Salt. Opinion is divided here – it's important not to salt anything to death, especially vegetables because of the impairment of flavour and so as not to consume too much sodium for health reasons. A light sprinkling with Maldon sea salt once cooked, however, brings out flavour. Unless specifically instructed to in the recipe, don't add salt to cooking water until it is bubbling as it will take a little longer to come to the boil.

Mediterranean Roasted Vegetables

These roasted vegetables are absolutely the taste of the summer holidays for me. They are easy to make and pretty versatile as you can serve them with rice, chops, sausages, spiced and roasted meats like lamb or chicken and couscous.

In roughly equal sized pieces, chop a variety of whatever Mediterranean type vegetables are to hand e.g. aubergine, courgette, pepper, fennel and onion. Place them in an oven proof dish, pour over a couple of tablespoons of olive oil, mix and season well with sea salt and black pepper, chopped garlic, dried oregano or fresh oregano and/or basil. Roast in a hot oven (200°C) for about an hour until the vegetables are cooked - caramelised but not burnt. Add some chopped sun blush or fresh tomatoes in the last 10 minutes for a kind of oven-baked ratatouille. I also like to add olives, fresh basil and crumbled feta before serving.

Winter Roasted Vegetables

These remind me of autumn; falling leaves, bonfire night suppers, harvest festivals and misty evenings.

In roughly equal sized pieces, chop a variety of winter vegetables e.g. carrots, swede, parsnip and butternut squash. Place them in an ovenproof dish, dot with a generous knob of butter and a splash of olive oil, season with fresh nutmeg and a sprinkle of caster sugar or a teaspoon of runny honey. Roast in a hot oven (200°C) for about an hour until the vegetables are cooked - caramelised but not burnt. Serve with rice, couscous and roasted meat like lamb and pork. Crumbled feta cheese or a few chilli flakes can add another flavour dimension.

Vegetable Mash and Purées

These make a lovely alternative to mashed potato, and you can use whatever is in season to ring the changes.

Peel and chop a mixture of carrot, swede and parsnip. Cut them into evenly sized chunks and add to a pan of boiling water. After about 10 to 15 minutes they should be cooked and tender. Drain and mash roughly with a knob of butter, sea salt and a good twist of pepper. I prefer white pepper in this, but black is also fine.

If you have a mouli, you can make a lovely, velvety vegetable purée with virtually any vegetable (broccoli, cauliflower, swede, carrot, celeriac, sweet potato, parsnip or, squash). However, the vegetables must be well cooked/steamed enough to force them through the blade. Make it richer by adding in concentrated chicken stock, melted butter, crème fraîche, cream or Greek yoghurt. This is excellent for weaning babies, as well as delighting adult diners.

Cauliflower Cheese

I love this on its own or served just with sausages or chops, but you can make a real feast of it by adding in a handful of chopped, cooked ham, some sautéed leeks or bacon and some cooked macaroni.

Rinse a large cauliflower in cold water, cut into florets and steam until just cooked for about 10 minutes (you can boil it, but it doesn't taste as nice). Drain and let the steam release from the florets. Mix with a quantity of my cheese sauce recipe and serve immediately.

You can also make a **cauliflower cheese gratin** by whizzing up some breadcrumbs, mixing them with a little olive oil and some grated Parmesan or Gruyère cheese, and then brown it under the grill.

Braised Red Cabbage

Aromatic, fruity and rich, this is the perfect companion for game like venison and wild boar, or with duck and goose. I usually make a large batch and freeze the rest so I can serve it without fuss, especially at Christmas. Most recipes for this contain sultanas, although I prefer chopped prunes to give it a rich flavour and silky texture.

Serves 4 to 6.
Equipment: Large cast iron ovenproof casserole, a mandolin makes light work of shredding the cabbage but a sharp chef's knife will do too.

Takes: 30 minutes to prep, 2 hours cooking

Ingredients
A medium sized red cabbage – approximately 900g, quartered and cored then finely shred
450g onions, chopped small
450g of cooking apples, peeled, cored and chopped
6 soft Agen style prunes, finely chopped
1 clove of finely chopped garlic
¼ whole freshly grated nutmeg
¼ level teaspoon ground cinnamon
3 tablespoons brown sugar
3 tablespoons red wine or cider vinegar
10g butter
Sea salt and freshly milled black pepper

Pre-heat the oven to 150°C
Prepare and chop the apple and onion, core and finely shred the cabbage. Layer the cabbage, onion and apple in the casserole and sprinkle in the garlic, spices and sugar.
Add the wine vinegar and butter, put the lid on the casserole and cook very slowly in the oven.
Add a handful of raisins, or finely stoned and chopped prunes for extra richness and contrast.
After about an hour, take it out of the oven and just stir it around to mix it all in thoroughly.
Put it back in the oven for another hour, season before serving.

Potatoes
What would we do without potatoes? Never mind the calories (you don't have to eat them every day), potatoes are just delicious, and so versatile. Potatoes come in many different varieties and are classed as either floury or waxy, which is all to do with the amount of dry matter they contain. They are graded on a scale of 1 to 10 with floury potatoes having more dry matter than waxy ones. Some are best for mashing, some for salads and so on. There's a great website called lovepotatoes.co.uk that has all kinds of fascinating information about the humble spud. Anyway, these are our regular family favourite recipes.

Irresistible Roasties

I don't know anyone who doesn't love roast potatoes. This recipe is always foolproof. Use good quality potatoes such as King Edwards's or Maris Piper, and goose or duck fat for the best flavour.

Preheat the oven to 200°C.
Peel and cut enough potatoes to provide at least three roasties per person. Keep them roughly even in size so that they all cook at the same rate.
Put them in cold water, bring to the boil, add a little salt and then parboil them for about 5 minutes.
Drain, keep them in the saucepan without the lid and allow the steam to dissipate for a few minutes. Then, shake them about a bit to rough up the edges. The rough edges help them to catch in the fat and crisp up. Either lightly dust them with a tablespoon of fine semolina (the best option) or plain flour.
Add four tablespoons of goose or duck fat (the tastiest option) or cooking oil into a baking tray, and put it into a hot oven around 200°C. Let the fat heat up, and then gently add the potatoes. I usually baste them a little before I put them back into the oven. Just to ring the changes, you can add a sprig of rosemary or a couple of crushed garlic cloves to flavour the cooking oil.
They will take about an hour to brown and crisp up. Don't take them out of the oven until you want to eat them if you want them to stay nice and crisp.

Mmmm, My Famous Creamy Mash

There's nothing more comforting than a pile of fluffy mash on a winter's day, especially if there's some fab gravy or delicious casserole sauce that needs mopping up. Buy good quality potatoes such as Vivaldi, Desiree or Maris Piper, always add the dairy ingredients in hot and follow my creaming method for the tastiest and most comforting kind of mash. Allow two medium sized potatoes per person, and as much butter, cream or semi skimmed milk etc. as your diet will allow.

Peel and cut the potatoes into even sized pieces, add them to boiling, salted water and cook until tender for about 10 to 15 minutes.
Drain and allow the steam to dissipate. For very smooth mash, but a little more effort, put the potatoes through a ricer, or just mash them thoroughly

with a potato masher to get rid of any lumps. Add a couple of tablespoons of hot milk or cream and a generous knob of butter. Then, whip them ***vigorously*** with a hand held whisk or a fork until really light and creamy. Don't overdo it, otherwise they will turn gluey instead of creamy.

Add sea salt and more butter, cream, crème fraîche or sour cream to taste. You can keep it warm for a while by keeping it in the saucepan. Put the lid on and stand it in another dish filled with boiling water from the kettle.

Variations

- Add a dessertspoon of capers, chives or pesto to serve with fish or chicken.
- Add whole grain mustard or sautéed leeks to serve with sausages or chops, or a spoonful of horseradish to serve with beef.
- Add lightly steamed, shredded cabbage to make colcannon.
- Mashed celeriac that has been cooked by being boiled with a clove of garlic and a dash of lemon juice (it stops it discolouring) in the water also makes it really special and light. If I add celeriac, I usually finish it with an electric whisk to get it really smooth.

New Potatoes

I could quite cheerfully eat a bowl of the first Jersey Royals all by themselves with nothing other than some melted butter. My Dad grows white skinned varieties (like Rocket and Pentland Javelin) that are also absolutely delicious and you just can't buy them that good in the shops. They are pretty easy to grow in a pot if you're so inclined, although I just like to make friends with generous home gardeners!

To prepare them, lightly scrub the potatoes (I use the rough side of a pan scourer, it's much easier) to remove any remaining soil. Leave the skins on and preferably cook them whole. Only cut them if they are not evenly sized, or some will cook more quickly than others. Place them into a pan of lightly salted, boiling water and a sprig of fresh mint. The mint is essential to bring out the flavor, in my humble opinion, and mint is very easy to grow in your garden or on a windowsill. They should cook in around 10 minutes. Drain and toss them in butter or olive oil and/or chopped fresh herbs such as parsley, or a finely chopped shallot.

Eat hot with pretty much anything – cold cuts, fish and salad. Save a few cold ones to make an open omelette, hash, or to fry up with a bit of oil and butter the next day topped with a poached egg. Use varieties such as Charlotte or Pink Fir Apple for potato salad.

Brilliant Baked Potatoes

Preheat the oven to 200°C. Scrub clean a good fluffy baking variety such as Maris Piper or King Edward. Prick each side with a fork, rub with a tiny bit of oil, sprinkle with a little sea salt, and bake in the oven on a baking tray for about an hour to hour and a half. The bigger the potato, the longer it will take. To speed things up, you can zap them in the microwave on high for 5 minutes first, and then finish them off in the oven for about 20 minutes. Remove from the oven and cut a cross in the top of the potato. Squeeze it gently from the bottom to open it and allow the steam to make it go fluffy. Use a tea towel to do this if you don't want to burn your hands. Top with butter, sour cream, grated cheese, chilli con carne or Bolognese sauce. A great meal on its own with a side salad, or served with sausages or chops.

Gratins

Preheat the oven to 160°C. Butter a shallow oven proof dish, rub generously with a cut clove of garlic, add layers of finely sliced potatoes whilst seasoning each layer with sea salt. The best varieties are the smooth types such as Desiree. Using a mandolin to cut the potatoes makes it easier, and the gratin will cook evenly because the slices are the same size. About 900g will easily fill a large dish. Rinse the slices in water to rinse off the starch and then dry them on a clean tea towel before layering them into the baking dish. Add the liquid – cream or stock (see below), and bake slowly for about an hour and a half. The top should go gloriously golden.

For a **gratin daupinois,** pour on a mixture of warmed half double cream, half milk (600 ml total).

Variations: Try adding alternate layers of **thinly sliced cauliflower** or **celeriac** in with the potatoes for a lighter and very tasty alternative. You could even make one with just thinly sliced parsnips, leave out the garlic and substitute a little grated nutmeg and a dash of chicken stock. It's very yummy.

Gratins can also be topped with grated cheese or a mixture of grated Parmesan and white or brown breadcrumbs to add extra texture.

Stock Bake or Boulanger Potatoes

Prepare the sliced potatoes as in the previous recipe using smooth varieties of potatoes such as Desiree or Estima. Pour on a pint of hot chicken stock (a cube will be fine) and a clove of finely crushed garlic, dot with a little extra butter. Bake in the oven for about an hour and half until golden and bubbling.

Hassleback Potatoes

Are these little hedgehog-like Swedish roast potatoes so-called because they are a bit a hassle to make? Anyway, if they are, they are still worth the effort. You will need even sized new potatoes, probably about 4 per person.

Pre-heat the oven to 200°C. Cut slices into the potatoes so they will absorb the cooking fat and fan out and turn golden like a roastie. Be careful not to cut all the way through the potato. To do that, place each one on a wooden spoon and cut 6 to 8 thin slices through each one. Heat a mixture of oil and butter in a roasting tin and thoroughly coat the potatoes in the oil. Make sure they are all cut sides up in the tray and sprinkle with salt (I quite like a little paprika sprinkled on them for a change), and roast them in the oven for about 40 minutes until cooked and golden.

Potato Wedges

First, heat the oven to 200°C.
Using fluffy varieties of potatoes such as King Edward, Desiree or Maris Piper, wash them thoroughly before cutting them vertically into chunks – 8 usually depending on the size of the potato. How many potatoes you use will depend on how many you are making per person or how greedy you are being :).

Parboil them in a large pan of boiling salted water for about 6 minutes (you don't want them to fall apart), then drain them and allow the steam to dissipate.
Put them in a large roasting dish so they can lay out flat and then toss them in enough vegetable or oil to coat them thoroughly.

To ring the changes, add different flavourings to the oil as follows or just add salt and pepper. Sesame seeds sprinkled over them are good too – nice and nutty. Bake in the oven for about 45 minutes.

Indian style: add a teaspoon of ground cumin, coriander, turmeric, a dash of cayenne pepper, salt and black pepper.

Spanish style: add a teaspoon of paprika or hot Pimenton to the oil.

Cajun style: a teaspoon of ground cumin, coriander and paprika. Salt and cracked black pepper and a pinch of dried oregano.

CHAPTER SIX: SAUCES, DRESSINGS & SEASONINGS

"A good upbringing means not that you won't spill sauce on the tablecloth, but that you won't notice it when someone else does".

Anton Chekhov
(Russian Dramatist)

A good sauce or dressing can make or break a meal. I've already given the recipe for some of the most useful ones in the sections where it makes sense to have them together, however, I've repeated some of them here just to make things as easy as possible for you to find them.

Chinese Sauce/Gravy
This is the sauce we use to dress our steamed pak choi when we make crispy pork.

4 teaspoons of sunflower oil
2 teaspoons of sesame oil
8 tablespoons of oyster sauce
2 tablespoons of dark soy sauce

Mix the ingredients in a small pan and just heat through before pouring over the steamed greens.

Roasted Onion Gravy
Delicious with any meat dish where there isn't a lot of meat stock such as toad in the hole.

Ingredients
2 large onions, peeled and sliced
2 teaspoons sunflower oil
1 teaspoon golden caster sugar
1 dessertspoon Worcestershire sauce
1 teaspoon mustard powder
1 dessertspoon plain flour

425 ml vegetable stock made from dissolving 1 1/2 teaspoons Marigold Swiss bouillon powder dissolved in boiling water.
Sea salt and freshly ground black pepper

Place the chopped onions, oil and sugar in a frying pan and mix thoroughly. Gently brown and caramelise the onions for about 20 minutes.
When they are ready, stir in the flour and allow it to cook through for a couple of minutes.
Boil a kettle and make the stock with the Marigold powder, mustard and Worcestershire sauce.
Gradually add in the stock to the onion mix and stir until smooth.
Bring to simmering point and cook for another 5 minutes. Taste to check the seasoning and pour into a warmed serving jug.

Horseradish Sauce

This is essential for serving with roast beef.
Mix half a jar of shop bought creamed horseradish with a tablespoon of crème fraîche for a light and delicious sauce to serve with roast beef. Serve at room temperature.

Apple Sauce

The perfect partner for roast pork.
Peel and core two Bramley cooking apples, place in a metal saucepan and add the juice of half a lemon. You can use dessert apples such as Cox's – they will need less sugar obviously. Cook gently on a medium heat on the hob for about 10 minutes until the apples turn fluffy. Turn off the heat and allow it to cool. Add sugar to taste. Some people add a knob of butter but it is perfectly nice without if you are calorie counting. A teaspoon of finely grated fresh ginger is a pleasant alternative and usually removes the need for much sugar. Serve slightly warm with roast pork.

Mint Sauce

Roast lamb wouldn't be the same without this sauce.

Mix two tablespoons of chopped fresh mint with 2 tablespoons of white wine vinegar (I find malt vinegar is far too strong), 1 tablespoon of water and a pinch of sugar. Adding a couple of very finely chopped spring onions can add a nice tang and extra texture for a change. Serve with roast lamb.

Bread Sauce
Perfect with roast chicken and turkey at Christmas.

Ingredients
2 small onions, peeled and each stuck with 2 cloves
1 bay leaf
4 peppercorns
A blade of mace or ¼ teaspoon ground mace
800ml whole milk
150g fresh white breadcrumbs
30g butter
2 tablespoons of double cream
Fresh nutmeg
A pinch of sea salt

Add the onions, milk, mace, peppercorns, a pinch of sea salt and bay leaves into a milk pan. Bring it to the boil; remove it from the heat, cover and leave to infuse for at least an hour. Strain the milk, put it back on a medium heat and sprinkle in the breadcrumbs. Cook for about 15 minutes - it should be quite thick by now. Just before serving, warm the butter and cream in another pan, grate a good dusting of nutmeg into it, and then stir into the bread sauce. Adjust the seasoning. Serve with roast chicken or turkey.

Mustard & Parsley Sauce
The sauce that boiled ham was made for!

Melt a generous knob of butter in a non-stick pan. Whisk in a couple of tablespoons of plain flour to make a roux. Cook gently for a few minutes and then gradually and carefully ladle in the hot gammon stock until you have a smooth thick sauce. Add a dessertspoon of Dijon mustard and some finely chopped fresh parsley. Serve with the gammon and extra vegetables. Heaven!

Essential Tomato Sauce

Served as a sauce for pasta it feeds 6-8 or, on meatballs or as a casserole base to serve 4 people comfortably. It freezes well, so make double and save a batch for another day.

Cook on the hob
Equipment: Thick bottomed, broad based pan
Takes: 10 minutes prep, cooks for 1 hour

Ingredients
1 large clove of garlic, crushed and finely chopped
4 tablespoons olive oil
1 teaspoon red chilli flakes
2 teaspoons dried oregano
3x 400g tins of preferably whole, un-chopped tomatoes
1 tablespoon of red wine or raspberry vinegar
Sea salt and ground black pepper to taste
Optional: fresh basil, roughly torn.
Optional: two or three finely chopped sun blush tomatoes.
Gently fry the garlic with the oil

Add the chilli, oregano and the tomatoes
Mix gently and leave the tomatoes whole until the end. Bring to the boil and gently simmer for about an hour. Add the vinegar, break up the tomatoes and add the rest of the olive oil. Season well to taste and add the fresh herbs.
Add to the pasta or meatballs as necessary.

Tubby Custard Sauce

You can't eat an apple pie or a crumble without a good helping of hot vanilla tubby custard. A non-stick milk saucepan is essential for this unless you really like scrubbing pans clean. You can make this the cheffy way with egg yolks, sugar and milk, but this is my easy cheat method and just as tasty.

Add 35g of Bird's custard powder and 20g of sugar to a heatproof basin. Mix to a smooth paste with a little cold milk. Heat 280ml of milk and the seeds from half a fresh vanilla pod (or a little vanilla bean paste), and then pour that on to the custard paste. It should go thick and smooth. Then add in about 300ml of whipped double cream. Stir and check for sweetness according to your taste.

White Sauces

White sauce is the cornerstone of a number of classic dishes. The key is to blend the flour and butter carefully and thoroughly so that the flour is cooked and the butter isn't allowed to go too dark. Practice makes perfect so try it a few times until you are happy with your technique. I always use a good quality non-stick milk saucepan and a silicone spoon and whisk – easier on the washing up and helps to avoid the sauce burning.

To make a basic white sauce with a roux of butter and flour and plain milk:
50g butter
50g plain flour
850 ml milk
Salt and ground white pepper

Melt the butter first and then stir in the flour with a wooden or silicone spoon and cook it gently on a low heat so it cooks without burning or colouring. Gradually add the milk into the roux. Switch to a whisk from a spoon now and whisk until you have a thick, creamy sauce. It will take 15 to 20 minutes. Straining will produce a smoother sauce if you've still got a few lumps in it.

Parsley Sauce

Make the basic white sauce as above, and then add freshly chopped English parsley to serve with boiled gammon or fish.

Cheese Sauce

Make as above add a large handful (175g) of grated strong cheese such as Cheddar and a generous pinch of English mustard powder.

Béchamel

A classic white sauce that can be used to top e.g. lasagne, although you may need to double the quantity if you are making a large one. The recipe is the same as for the other white sauces but the milk is flavoured beforehand using 1 small onion, 1 bay leaf, 1 small carrot and 1 sprig of parsley. Put the milk, carrot, parsley, bay leaf and onion in a non-stick milk pan and bring to the boil. Leave it to stand and infuse for an hour, strain and then add gradually to the butter and flour roux until you have a smooth sauce.

For topping **Moussaka** – use the recipe above and whip the yolks of two eggs into it so that it sets like custard when cooked.

Fresh Mayonnaise

Homemade mayo will keep in a screw top jar the fridge for up to 1 week and tastes a million times better than shop bought, mass produced brands. Make it once to see how easy it is, and then you'll make it all the time.

Ingredients
2 egg yolks at room temperature
1 teaspoon of Dijon mustard
1 crushed clove of garlic (optional)
300 ml groundnut or sunflower oil
2 teaspoons of cider or white wine vinegar
Pinch of salt and ground white pepper

In a bowl mix the egg yolk, garlic and mustard together with a wooden spoon. Using an electric hand whisk, keep mixing while you add the oil one drop at a time until it starts to thicken. Once it is past this critical stage where it might split you can continue to add a thin, steady stream of oil until it is all added. Stir in the vinegar until the consistency looks right and add the seasoning. If it splits, just crack another egg yolk into a clean bowl, add the split mixture one drop at a time until it's all absorbed and then continue with the rest of the oil.

Tartare Sauce
Serve with grilled or fried fish.
250 ml mayonnaise
1 tablespoon of finely chopped capers

2 tablespoons finely chopped cornichons (gherkins)
1 tablespoon of finely chopped shallot
Salt and pepper
Tabasco to taste

Mix everything together and season well and spoon into a serving bowl.

Aioli

Serve with lots of lovely fresh, raw vegetables, hardboiled eggs and salami.

4 cloves of garlic with the green centre removed
2 egg yolks
450 ml good quality plain olive oil (not extra virgin, it's too bitter) or groundnut oil
Juice of a lemon
Salt and pepper

Crush the garlic in to a mortar and pestle, whisk in the egg yolks. Drizzle the oil in, stirring constantly until you have a thick yellow mayonnaise. Stir in the lemon juice and season to taste.

Top tip. If your mayo starts to split (usually because you've added the oil in too quickly), add another egg yolk into a clean bowl and beat the mixture back into it and then continue adding the rest of the oil.

Blender Hollandaise

Delicious served with white fish, poached chicken or Eggs Benedict.

500g unsalted butter
4 eggs
Juice of a medium lemon
Pinch of white pepper

Melt the butter in a pan that has a pouring lip. Put the eggs, lemon juice and pepper into your blender or food processor. Pour the hot melted butter evenly into the eggs as they are being whisked until the sauce thickens. Keep it warm over a pan of freshly boiled water until you want to serve it. Add other herbs such as finely chopped mint, blanched sorrel or tarragon as you like.

Béarnaise Sauce
This is great with chicken or steak.

Put 1 tablespoon of chopped tarragon, 2 finely chopped shallots, ground black pepper and 50 ml white wine vinegar into a small pan. Boil it rapidly until it reduces to 1 tablespoon. Stir into a quantity of Hollandaise.

Beurre Blanc
This is perfect with white fish.

50g shallots, very finely chopped
2 tablespoon of white wine vinegar
4 tablespoon of dry white wine or vermouth such as Noilly Prat.
6 tablespoons water
2 tablespoons double cream
175 g chilled unsalted butter cut into small pieces.

Put the shallots, vinegar, wine and water into a pan and simmer until it's reduced to about 4 tablespoons. Add the cream and boil until reduced a little more. Lower the heat and gradually whisk in the pieces of butter, a few pieces at a time until it is thick and creamy. Season to taste with salt and pepper.

Essential Salad Dressing
Home made salad dressing is so much nicer than shop bought and you know what is in it i.e. no unnecessary thickeners or additives.

1 tablespoon of white wine vinegar
4 tablespoons of olive oil
¼ teaspoon of caster sugar
Pinch of sea salt

Place the ingredients in a jar and shake until thoroughly mixed. Dress any green salad with it.

Variation: Use red wine vinegar instead of white and add a tablespoon of finely chopped shallots for a tasty tomato salad – especially good served with steak.

Vinaigrette Salad Dressing

It's a classic French dressing so I always use French mustard.

Mix 1 teaspoon of white wine vinegar with 1 teaspoon of Dijon mustard. Then mix in 5 or 6 teaspoons of olive oil. Season to taste.

Variations: Add chopped fresh herbs such as tarragon or chives to ring the changes, or use different oil, mustard and vinegar mixes. Truffle vinegar and walnut oil is my current favourite mix to dress crisp green salad leaves that have been sprinkled with a few sesame seeds.

Persillade

Use to sprinkle on a casserole to give a fresh lift just before serving.

Finely chop 2 peeled garlic cloves and 20 g flat parsley and mix it together. Adding finely chopped fresh mint to the mixture is great for sprinkling on a spring lamb stew.

Thai Green Curry Paste

This paste gives the classic Thai taste to curries and stir-fries, and the ingredients are all readily available in supermarkets these days.

5 fat lemongrass stalks, chopped
2 medium-hot green chillies
25g peeled fresh ginger
3 fat garlic cloves
50g chopped shallots
½ teaspoon of sea salt
1 teaspoon of shrimp paste

Put all the ingredients in a mini food processor with 3 tablespoons of water and blitz it to a smooth paste. Make a double batch and freeze what you don't use for another time.

Aromatic Curry Powder

2 tablespoons of coriander seeds
2 tablespoons of fenugreek seeds
1 tablespoon of mustard seeds
1 teaspoon of cumin seeds
½ teaspoon fennel seeds
1 teaspoon black peppercorns
1 cinnamon stick, broken into pieces
3 cloves
1 tablespoon of ground turmeric

Put all the spices in an electric coffee grinder (I keep one just for spices) and keep in a screw top jar or an airtight plastic tub and use as and when you need it.

Garam Masala

A sprinkle of this in a curry adds an extra touch of sweetness and fragrance. Most Indian families have their own recipe for this. Store it in a screw-top glass jar and keep it in a draw or cupboard away from the sunlight.

2 teaspoon of cardamom seeds – about 30 green pods
1 teaspoon of cloves
2 medium sized cinnamon sticks, broken into smaller pieces
4 large pieces of blade mace
4 tablespoons of cumin seeds
2 tablespoons of coriander seeds
1 tablespoon of black peppercorns

Heat up a small heavy-based frying pan, add the whole spices and heat them up for a few moments to bring out the flavour but don't let them burn. Grind them to a fine powder in a spice/coffee grinder.

CHAPTER SEVEN: PASTA

"The trouble with eating Italian food is that five or six days later you're hungry again".
George Miller
(American stand-up comedian)

Most Italians eat pasta as just one course, whereas we tend to eat it as a meal in itself. Hmmm, maybe that explains our weight problems! Either way, the trick is to buy good quality pasta made of high quality durum wheat and keep the sauces simple and appropriate to the shape of pasta that you're eating. Fresh tagliatelle noodles, lasagne and ravioli are delicious when eaten made with fresh egg pasta – it takes practice but making your own can be fun and tastes delicious. For everything else, dried pasta such as farfalle, rigatoni, macaroni and linguine are perfectly fine. Barilla is my favourite everyday brand and most supermarket and delis sell a variety of artisan brands these days.

One last tip - always remember to put your serving dishes on to warm *before* you begin cooking so that your pasta doesn't go cold really quickly once served.

Fresh Egg Pasta Dough

Once you've made this a few times, you'll realise it's pretty easy, very tasty and will make you feel very pleased with yourself!

600g Tipo '00' fine Italian flour
6 eggs or 12 egg yolks (the better the eggs the better tasting the pasta) – lightly whisked

Place the flour on a board, make a well, pour the eggs into the middle and mix together with the flour to make a dough. Flour your hands and knead until you have smooth, silky, elastic dough. Cover with clingfilm and leave it to rest in the fridge for half an hour.
Roll it as thinly as possible using a pasta machine. The thinner it's rolled, the better it tastes.

Cut the dough into manageable chunks.
Set it to the widest setting first and pass it through, folding and re-folding about 10 times to finish the kneading process.
Gradually reduce the setting width, and then keep passing it through until it is thin enough. Clear your kitchen table, sprinkle some fine semolina on it and lay the sheets out on it to dry it out a little before cutting.
Repeat the process with your remaining dough. After it has been drying for about 10-15 minutes, cut into the shapes you want – lasagne sheets, tagliatelle, ravioli etc., and cook according to your recipe.

Lasagne

I love homemade lasagne but it does take a while to prepare so, when I make it, I make a big one!

Serves 4
Can be cooked on the hob and finished off in the oven
Equipment: large rectangular oven proof dish
Time: 20 minutes, plus 25 minutes to cook

Ingredients

1 quantity of Anna's Bolognese sauce as follows
1 pack of fresh lasagne sheets - these are often best soaked in a little warm water for about 10 minutes beforehand. If you use dried lasagne sheets, pre-soaking is essential and needs to be factored into the prep time.
1 quantity of béchamel sauce – 2 tablespoons of flour, a knob of butter, 1 pint of semi-skimmed milk, a onion, a couple of bay leaves, 3 or flour cloves
Grated Parmesan

Make the Bolognese sauce as in the next recipe.
Once the sauce has gone into oven, push the cloves into the onion, put it into a non-stick milk saucepan place with the milk, bay leaves and the cloves and bring to the boil. As soon as it boils, take it off the heat and leave to infuse for about an hour.
Just before the Bolognese sauce is ready, you can make the béchamel sauce.
Pre-heat the oven to 200°C.
Take the onion and bay leaves out of the milk.
Melt the butter in a saucepan over a gentle heat.
Stir in the flour with a wooden spoon and mix to a smooth paste. Let it

cook for a few moments.
Start to add the milk gradually, making sure it has been absorbed into the butter and flour paste with a whisk. Keep adding the milk and whisking gently until you have a thick, creamy sauce.
Set it aside and then start to assemble the lasagne.
Butter the baking dish and start layering the Bolognese sauce, then sheets of lasagne. You should keep going with a couple of layers, finishing with a layer of lasagne. Pour the béchamel sauce over the top, sprinkle on some grated Parmesan and put into the oven for about 30 minutes.
It takes about 30 minutes for the lasagne to cook through, and for the top layer to go nice and brown.
Remove from the oven and allow it to rest for a few minutes before serving.
Serve with a side salad or simple tomato salad.

Favourite Pasta Sauces

Any pasta, especially the fresh kind that you make yourself, can be just delicious dressed with a fruity olive oil, grated Parmesan and chopped fresh soft leaf herbs such as basil.

Anna's Bolognese Sauce

This can be used to coat your favourite type of pasta, or as the basis for a lasagne. This recipe is inspired by one made by our Italian friend, Anna, that we used to eat when we were on holiday in Rome. The meat needs to be very finely ground if you want the sauce to stick to pasta like spaghetti. For laundry reasons, I usually eat it with penne!

Serves 4
Cooks on the hob
Equipment: oven-proof casserole that can also be used on the hob or a saucepan
Time: 20 minutes, plus 40 minutes to cook - the longer, the better

Ingredients
450g of good quality ground or minced beef from a butcher
2 finely chopped rashers of unsmoked bacon or pancetta
2 tablespoons of concentrated tomato paste
1 tablespoon of olive oil and a knob of butter

1 onion, a stick of celery and a carrot all very finely chopped
1 bay leaf
A teaspoon of good quality dried oregano or a pack of fresh marjoram or oregano
4 tablespoons of red wine
Sea salt and freshly milled black pepper and a touch of grated nutmeg
150ml meat stock
150ml whole milk
Your favourite pasta – penne, linguine, farfalle etc.

Finely chop the bacon, onions, celery and carrot.
Heat the oil and butter in whatever pan you are using.
Add the vegetables and bacon to the oil and cook gently for about 5 minutes until softened.
Turn up the heat, add the minced beef and stir until nicely browned.
Add the tomato paste, wine, bay leaf, oregano, sea salt and pepper, the meat stock and milk.
Stir and either leave to simmer gently on the hob for 40 minutes until the meat is tender and the sauce is nice and thick or cook in the oven for about 45 minutes.
Pasta usually takes between 3 and 10 minutes to cook so get the kettle boiling and set the pan of pasta on to coincide with when the sauce is ready. Drain the pasta and mix thoroughly with the hot meat sauce, or set aside to use for your lasagne.

Essential Tomato Sauce or 'Sugo'
As a pasta sauce it feeds 6-8
Cook on the hob
Equipment: Thick bottomed, broad based pan
Takes: 10 minutes prep, cooks for 1 hour

Ingredients
1 large clove of garlic, crushed and finely chopped
4 tablespoons olive oil
1 teaspoon red chilli flakes
2 teaspoons dried oregano
3 400g tins of preferably whole, tomatoes
Optional: two or three finely chopped Sunblush tomatoes
1 tablespoon of red wine or raspberry vinegar
Sea salt and ground black pepper to taste

Optional: fresh basil, roughly torn.

Gently fry the garlic with the oil
Add the chilli, oregano and the tomatoes
Mix gently and leave the tomatoes whole until the end. Bring to the boil and then turn down the heat and gently simmer for about an hour. Add the vinegar, break up the tomatoes and add the rest of the olive oil. Season well to taste and add the fresh herbs. Add to the pasta as appropriate.

Sugo with Chorizo

The ingredients are the same as above plus 50g of chopped and fried chorizo. Follow the same recipe as above.

Sugo Puttanesca

The ingredients are the same as for the sugo recipe above, but with the additional of a tablespoon of capers and chopped black and green olives.

Sugo Siciliana

This is my favourite of all the pasta sauces, especially with a nice glass of smoky red wine. Cut an aubergine or two into slices and then again into finger sized pieces and fry them in olive oil, or roast them in larger slices on a griddle and then cut them into fingers. Once they are golden, add them to the sugo sauce. Cook your spaghetti and then add the sauce. Serve with crumbled feta cheese and torn basil leaves.

Sugo Gambero

Make the sugo, then add raw peeled prawns to the sauce. Serve with a garnish of chopped fresh mint.

Creamy Mushroom Sauce

This is one of my favourites with fresh tagliatelle noodles.

200 g mushrooms (wild, cultivated or a mixture of both), chopped
A knob of butter

150 ml double cream
1 clove of peeled garlic crushed into a paste
200g of pasta such as linguine, tagliatelle or farfalle

Cook the pasta according to the instructions on the pack in boiling salted water.
Sauté the mushrooms in a frying pan using the butter and garlic paste, add the cream and season to taste.
Drain the pasta, put the pan back on to the heat and stir in the mushroom and cream mixture.
Serve on heated plates or pasta bowls. Finish with a little shredded basil or chopped parsley.

Spicy Sausage & Mustard

This is sooooo tasty and quite sophisticated enough for a lunch or supper dish.

Serves 4
Equipment: saucepan for the pasta and a large frying pan
Takes: 10 minutes prep, 20 minutes to cook

Ingredients
400g coarse pork sausagemeat
1 large banana shallot – finely chopped
Large glass of dry white wine
Generous pinch of chilli flakes
2 tablespoons of Dijon mustard
350ml double cream
Fresh thyme leaves to garnish and add a fresh flavour
1 tablespoon of olive oil
Ground black pepper and salt
Pasta to serve four – shells or tube shapes

Put the water on to boil and start cooking the pasta.
Heat the oil in a pan and gently sauté the chopped shallot.
Crumble in the sausage meat, let it sizzle and cook through.
Stir in the chilli, the mustard and the cream.

Adjust the seasoning.
Drain the pasta and add it to the hot sauce.
Serve hot and sprinkle with fresh thyme leaves.

Variation: replace the mustard with 1 teaspoon of coarsely ground fennel seeds and add 150ml of chicken stock and 150ml of dry white wine to the sauce.

Pesto Sauce

Delicious when used to dress silky pasta like linguine, to make a tasty summer salad with cooked risotto rice, or used as a stuffing for a piece of chicken thigh meat wrapped in proscutto and oven baked until crispy.

Serves 4.
Equipment: Mini-blender
Takes: 10 minutes

Ingredients
50g fresh basil leaves
25g grated Parmesan
1 clove of garlic, crushed
1 large tablespoon of pine nuts (my little top tip - keep what you don't use in the freezer – they'll stay fresher longer and have such a high fat content that they don't need defrosting)
Olive oil
Sea salt and ground black pepper

Put all the ingredients except the cheese and salt into a mini blender, and blitz into a smooth purée. Then add the cheese.
If you don't have blender, use a mortar and pestle instead (the traditional method actually - it just takes a bit of extra elbow grease). Pound the basil, garlic and pine kernels to a paste (adding a little abrasive sea salt makes it easier), add the oil gradually and then the cheese. Season to taste.

Carbonara

Such a delicious dish, it's fast and fabulous so make sure your plates are warmed, not that it will hang around for long!

Serves 4
Cook on the hob
Equipment - a frying pan, a saucepan and a small mixing bowl
Takes: 5 minutes prep, 5 minutes to cook

Ingredients
110g pancetta or streaky bacon, cut into lardons
2 tablespoons of olive oil
350g dried spaghetti or linguine
Sea salt and black pepper
6 large eggs
50ml water
Three tablespoons of freshly grated Parmesan cheese

Cook the lardons in hot oil until just crisping and put the pan to one side.
Cook the spaghetti or linguine in plenty of boiling salted water.
Beat the eggs with the water, season them well with salt and ground black pepper, add two tablespoons of the Parmesan.
When the spaghetti is ready, drain it well and return it to the pan.
Add in the lardons as well as the pancetta flavoured oil from the pan and toss it into the pasta thoroughly.
Now add the egg mixture and dress the pasta with it until the sauce thickens. If it doesn't thicken, return the pan to the heat, but only for a few seconds or the mixture will scramble.
Serve in warm dishes with the remaining grated Parmesan.

Cheat's Cannelloni

I call this a cheat because you can use fresh lasagne sheets from a deli (you could make this yourself if you have time on your hands), and use a short cut cream sauce. It's a great family dish as it goes a long way. Use well-flavoured fillings and be generous with the sauce. Delicious with a green salad as a side dish.

Serves 4
Equipment: a large rectangular ovenproof baking dish (18 x 23cm)
Takes: 40 minutes prep, 40 minutes to cook

Ingredients

Fresh lasagne sheets - cut each sheet one in half to make the tubes
Béchamel sauce (as per the lasagne recipe) or (to cheat) mix a 500ml tub of crème fraîche with 100g of Parmesan cheese with a pinch of salt and white pepper
1 quantity of basic tomato sauce
Cheese for grating over the top, either provolone or mozzarella and Parmesan

Favourite fillings

Brassica and anchovy. Mix together 500g of chopped, steamed broccoli and cauliflower, 25g tinned anchovies with the oil, and 2 crushed cloves of garlic, a pinch of dried chilli flakes, salt and pepper. Cook it together in a frying pan and cook it down slowly for about 20 minutes until it is paste-like enough to be rolled into the lasagne sheets.

Beef and tomato. Use a quantity of the meatball mixture as per the Marvellous Meatball recipe.

Leek and ricotta. Finely slice 3 medium leeks (900g) and cook them gently, uncovered, on the hob with 2 cloves of crushed garlic, 2 teaspoons of fresh thyme leaves and 2 tablespoons of water. When they are tender, and all the liquid has evaporated, let them cool and then mix with 250g of ricotta cheese and season to taste with salt and pepper.
Pre-heat the oven to 180°C.
Butter the baking dish.
Lay each pasta sheet on a chopping board and spoon a sausage-like line of filling into each one. Fill them evenly.
Roll them into cannelloni shaped tubes and place each one seam-side down into the dish.
When the dish is full, cover the pasta with the tomato sauce and then the white sauce.
Sprinkle with the cheese and bake in the oven on a baking sheet for 40 minutes, or until golden and bubbling. Remove it from the oven and let it cool for about 10 minutes before serving.

Pasta, Ham & Peas

This is just delicious with home cooked ham and it takes no time at all to prepare. I saw Nigella Lawson make this on one of her early TV programmes for her children for supper and it's been one of our favourites ever since.

Serves four
400g pasta shapes – bow shapes (Farfalle) work best
200g frozen petits pois
300 ml double cream
300g chopped, cooked ham (preferably leftovers from your own cooked gammon)
3 tablespoons grated Parmesan

Cook the pasta according to the instructions on the pack in boiling salted water. Just before it's ready add the frozen peas. Drain and then put the pan back on the heat. Stir in the ham, cream and Parmesan and warm it through. Serve on warmed plates.

Mac n'Cheese

A real comfort food pasta classic, I like this served by itself with a few slices of tomato on the side (or a few baked cherry tomatoes on the vine), with sausages, or sprinkled with some chopped home baked ham. Or sliced leeks cooked in butter. Or with fried bacon. So many delicious possibilities!

Serves 4
Equipment: Non-stick pan for the cheese sauce, saucepan for cooking the macaroni, large baking dish to serve.
Takes: 30 minutes

Ingredients
350g macaroni or penne
Cheese sauce
50g butter
50g plain flour
850 ml milk
200g strong Cheddar cheese, grated
Salt and ground white pepper
Pinch of English mustard powder

Melt the butter, stir in the flour and cook it gently on a low heat so it cooks without burning or colouring.
Gradually add the milk into the roux, whisk until you have a thick, creamy

sauce. It will take about 15 minutes.
Add in the cheese and let it melt and the mustard powder, salt and ground white pepper.
Taste for seasoning and adjust to your taste.
Put the water for the pasta on to boil, salt it and cook according to the directions on the pack.
Combine the cooked drained pasta with the cheese sauce.

WHAT'S4TEAMUM?

CHAPTER EIGHT: SEAFOOD

"I will not eat oysters. I want my food dead - not sick, not wounded – dead".
Woody Allen
(American film director, comedian, actor, writer)

When it comes to seafood, as with most dishes, good quality ingredients and simple treatments are usually the best options. I don't use many recipes for fish as such because I normally just buy what's fresh and available, pan fry it in some oil and butter, steam it or bake it in the oven.

Some people won't cook fresh fish because they don't like touching it, or they just don't know how to prepare it. If that's you, just ask your fishmonger to fillet or descale it for you.

Spicy Prawns with Courgettes

I've been making this dish for years., it's not only delicious and fresh tasting, it's also relatively low in calories. Double joy!

Serves 4
Equipment: a wok or non-stick frying pan and a flat-bottomed pan for the rice
Takes: 15 minutes prep, cooks in 10 minutes

Ingredients

4 courgettes, washed with ends sliced off and cut into 2 cm chunks and then again into 4 smaller chunks
350 g good quality medium to large, raw prawns
2 tablespoons of sunflower oil
4 cloves of garlic, finely chopped
1 fresh, hot green chilli, seeds removed, finely chopped
½ teaspoon turmeric
¼ teaspoon chilli powder
1½ teaspoons of ground cumin
1 teaspoon of finely grated fresh ginger
1 teaspoon ground coriander
1 400 g tin tomatoes
1 tablespoon lemon juice

2 large handfuls coriander, freshly chopped
Basmati rice

As with all stir-fry recipes, it is important to prepare and set aside all the ingredients before you start as this cooks very quickly. Measure out all the spices and set them out together on a small plate.
Start cooking the rice - this is very fast food indeed (see the rice section for the best way to cook).
Put the oil in your pan, add the garlic and switch the hob to high (cooking the garlic in cold oil as it warms up stops it tasting bitter). Just let it sizzle for a few moments and be careful not to let it go brown and burn.
Add the courgettes, turmeric and cumin and just fry them off in the oil for a few moments.
Add the chilli, ginger, tomatoes and lemon juice.
Stir to mix and simmer for a few minutes to evaporate off the liquid so you are left with a thick sauce.
Add the prawns and coriander to just warm and cook through for 3 minutes or so.
Remove from the heat and serve with plain basmati rice.

Cod with Spicy Tomato Sauce

This is a really tasty and colourful fish dish. We like it served with basmati rice with peas.

Serves 4
Equipment: 2 non-stick frying pans, an oven proof baking dish and a flat-bottomed pan for the rice
Takes: 10 minutes prep, cooks in 30 minutes. Cook on the hob and finish in the oven

Ingredients
1 900g cod loin or 4 cod steaks (it's also great with salmon)
1 ½ teaspoons of salt
½ teaspoon of cayenne pepper
¼ teaspoon of turmeric
8 tablespoons of vegetable oil
1 teaspoon of whole fennel seeds
1 teaspoon of whole mustard seeds
2 teaspoons of ground cumin seeds

200g onions, finely chopped
2 cloves of garlic, finely chopped
1 400g tin of chopped tomatoes
¼ teaspoon of garam masala
Pre-heat the oven to 180°C.
Butter the baking dish.

Rub the fish with half the salt and cayenne pepper, all of the turmeric and a little oil.
Make the sauce by adding 4 tablespoons of oil to your pan and when it's hot, add the fennel and mustard seeds.
When they start to pop, add the onions and garlic and fry until they brown lightly.
Add the ground cumin, remaining salt and cayenne.
Add the tomatoes and garam masala, bring to the boil, turn it down and simmer for 15 minutes.
Place the fish in the baking dish – skin side down, pour over the tomato sauce and bake uncovered for 15 minutes.

Baked Salmon or White Fish

Hot or cold, this is a 'quick to make', all year round favourite. Buy the best quality salmon or firm fleshed white fish such as hake or cod.

Serves 4
Cook in the oven at 150°C
Equipment: baking foil or parchment to make an individual parcel for each piece of fish and a baking sheet
Takes: 5 minutes prep, cooks in 8 minutes.

Ingredients
4 salmon, hake or cod fillets – thoroughly descaled and pin boned
Knob of butter or a dash of olive oil
Optional: slice of lemon per fillet, sprig of dill, sautéed onion or fennel, cherry tomatoes.

Butter four pieces of foil or parchment big enough for each piece of fish. Add the fish and the combination of flavourings/ ingredients you want – dot with butter. Make each one into a tight parcel so that it can cook in its own steam.

Place on a baking tray and place in a pre-heated oven for about 8 minutes. Remove from the oven, take the fish and all the lovely sauce and put it on a warmed plate - serve with rice or creamed potato and green vegetables like peas, broad beans, broccoli or buttered spinach.

Pancetta Wrapped Cod

The pancetta and cod (or hake) combination make this tasty and attractive enough for a dinner party or family supper dish. Smoky ham and white fish make for very tasty bedfellows. You could use Parma ham instead of the pancetta.

Serves 4
Equipment: frying pan and a baking dish
Takes: 30 minutes, start on the hob, finish in the in the oven.

Ingredients
4 pieces of cod (or hake) with the scales scrubbed off
Pack of thinly sliced pancetta.
1 tablespoon of olive oil

Pre-heat the oven to 160°C.
Wrap the pancetta around the cod.
Heat the oil in the pan and fry it on both sides for 3 minutes until lightly browned.
Transfer to the oven on a greased ovenproof dish for about 10 minutes.
Serve with crushed new potatoes or Puy lentils and wilted, buttered spinach.

Asian Tuna

Fresh tuna has a very meaty texture so it can take the savoury flavours of Asian cooking very well. I like this so much that sometimes I struggle to get it as far as the noodles!

Serves 4
Cook on the hob
Equipment: a wok or frying pan
Takes: 10 minutes prep, cooks in 10 minutes

Ingredients
4 tuna steaks
4 dessertspoons of light soy sauce mixed with a dessertspoon of olive oil.
2 dessertspoons of sesame seeds
Asian salad – finely cut 'julienne' strips of courgette, carrot, cucumber, bean shoots and blanched French beans with a rice wine and sesame oil dressing.

Marinate the fish in the oil and soy mixture for at least an hour. Heat a lightly oiled pan and dip the tuna steaks in sesame seeds before frying them lightly on each side. This is better with the tuna left pink inside. Serve with an Asian salad and noodles.

Lowestoft Fish Pie

I always used to be a Delia fish pie fan and then I discovered Jamie's Fantastic Fish Pie. These days, I prefer to mix it up a bit and model it on the one they serve at Wheelers as well. Make it with the fresh catch of the day and it will be delicious however you make it.

Serves 4
Cook on the hob and finish in the oven
Equipment: A saucepan for the mash, a sauté pan and a large ceramic ovenproof dish
Takes: 25 minutes prep, 30 minutes to cook

Ingredients
500g white fish such as cod with a little smoked haddock. A little salmon and prawns make a nice change but white fish on its own is pretty delicious
150g of fresh spinach (omit this if you'd rather serve it with green vegetables on the side)
2 hard-boiled eggs, quartered
Juice of a lemon
250ml double cream
1 stick of celery, finely chopped
One banana shallot, finely chopped
1 large handful of parsley, finely chopped
1 heaped teaspoon of Dijon mustard
Cheese

Topping

900g freshly boiled potatoes
A tablespoon of olive oil
A little freshly grated nutmeg
25g grated Cheddar cheese
Salt and freshly ground pepper

Pre-heat the oven to 220°C.
Put the potatoes for the topping on to boil in salted water and cook until tender. Once cooked, drain, let the steam rise off them. Mash until smooth; whip in the olive oil with a fork and season with nutmeg. Cover and keep warm until the pie needs topping.
Hard-boil the eggs, let them cool and then shell and quarter them.
Wilt the spinach and squeeze out any excess moisture.
Lightly butter the serving dish.
Sauté the shallot and celery in the butter. Take it off the heat; add the cream, chopped parsley, lemon juice and mustard.
Cut the fish into bite sized chunks and layer them in the base of the baking dish.
Tuck the pieces of hard-boiled in amongst the fish, layer the wilted spinach over it and pour the sauce over it.
Spoon the potato over the fish and sauce, cover with cheese and place on a baking sheet in the oven.
Cook until golden.
It can be dish by itself but add some peas if you wish. I prefer to leave out the spinach if serving with green veg such as cabbage, broccoli or peas.

Moules Marinière à la Crème

This is a 'Stickman' signature dish and one of the very first things he ever cooked for me when we met, many years ago. I have never made this myself because it's nice to keep some things special that only he makes – I assure you that it is completely delicious! The one thing you need to be absolutely clear about is that the wine must be Muscadet as anything else really doesn't taste as good!

Serves 4 as a main course
Cook on the hob
Equipment: a very large cooking pot with a lid
Takes: 60 minutes to prep, 10 minutes to cook

Ingredients

1/2 kilo of rope grown mussels per person – thoroughly cleaned
50g butter and a dash of sunflower oil
1 clove of garlic
2-3 banana shallots, finely chopped
1 bottle of Muscadet white wine – use 150 ml to cook, drink the rest!
3 tablespoons of double cream
Ground white pepper
Large bunch of parsley, finely chopped
French bread cut into rounds

Buying rope grown mussels means they are likely to be very clean, but they must be used on the day they are bought because shellfish spoils very quickly. As soon as you get them home, put them in a sink of cold water. Throw away any that float to the top. Leave the cold tap running, use a small knife and scrape off all the little hairy beards and barnacles. Discard any that are broken. If any are open, give them a sharp tap with a knife. If they don't close immediately, throw them away. If you buy non rope-grown mussels, it is essential that you put them into clean water after cleaning and change it two or three times as this will clear any remaining grit in them. Leave in the cold water until you're ready to cook them.

In a large pan, melt the butter and oil over a low heat and then gently cook the chopped shallot and garlic for about 5 minutes. Be careful not let them brown.

Drain and dry the mussels.

Add the white wine and cream to the pan and, when it comes to simmering temperature, tip in the mussels and cover with the lid so they can cook in the steam – this will take 4 or 5 minutes.

Remove the lid and start lifting the mussels out with a slotted spoon as they open. Put them in a warm serving dish. Throw away any that didn't open during the cooking process.

Pour the remaining sauce into a serving jug.

Get everyone to the table and ready to eat. Sprinkle the mussels in the serving bowl with some parsley, cut the French bread into small rounds for soaking up the lovely sauce.

Give everyone their own bowl to help themselves to mussels and sauce and provide a large, spare bowl for the empty shells and lots of napkins. Serve the remaining wine with this and expect to eat without much conversation – this is a meal that everyone loves to completely get into!

Sharon's Southwold Smoked Salmon Pâté

This is delicious as a starter with Melba toast, good quality brown bread or soda bread. Serve in a single dish and let everyone help themselves, or in individual ramekins. My friend Sharon made this for us as a New Year's Eve supper party starter in Southwold a few years back - I begged her for the recipe!

Ingredients
170g smoked salmon trimmings (or half salmon, half smoked trout)
255g of cream cheese
150 ml double cream
1 tablespoon of chopped chives or dill
30g butter
½ teaspoon of cayenne pepper
1 teaspoon of creamed horseradish
Juice of a lemon
Freshly ground black pepper
Capers to serve

Put the fish, cream cheese and double cream into a blender.
Add the butter, cayenne, horseradish, lemon juice and seasoning.
Blend it to a rough paste – I prefer a bit of texture but you may want it smoother. If so, pass it through a flat sieve.
Sprinkle it with capers, a little cayenne pepper or a sprig of dill.
Allow it to set in the fridge before serving.

Smoked Mackerel Pâté
Make as above, but substitute fillets of smoked mackerel for the smoked salmon and leave out the dill. I like to serve it with capers or dill cucumber spears.

Melba Toast
Simply toast medium-thick slices of white bread under a medium high grill until they are lightly golden on both sides. Put onto a board and slice off the crusts, then put your hand on top of each slice in turn and cut across into quarters. Grill them again for a few more seconds until crisp and golden. Remove from the grill and leave to cool

CHAPTER NINE: SALADS

"To make a good salad is also how to be a brilliant diplomat - the problem is entirely the same in both cases. To know how much oil one must mix with one's vinegar."
Oscar Wilde
(Anglo-Irish playwright, novelist, poet)

Salade Niçoise

There are many dishes that remind me of sunny, Mediterranean holidays but this has to be my favourite. I also serve this as a summer lunch for the girls – it always goes down a storm. It feels so healthy and light, we can then eat a yummy pud with a clear conscience!

Serves 2

Ingredients
New potatoes - 8 smallish ones, boiled or steamed and cut into thick coins then dressed with olive oil, salt and pepper
8 cherry tomatoes
2 seared tuna steaks or a drained tin of tuna in brine
2 eggs boiled for 6 minutes, shelled and quartered lengthwise
A good handful of green beans blanched i.e. cooked in hot water for a few minutes and then rinsed with cold water
2 dessertspoons of capers
8 silver-skinned anchovies
Little gem lettuce
Vinaigrette dressing

Dress the salad ingredients (lettuce, beans and tomatoes) in the dressing and arrange equally on 2 plates. Then arrange the eggs, potatoes, anchovies and tunas on the plate and sprinkle with capers.

Celeriac Remoulade

Mustardy and crunchy, this is gorgeous with cold meats. I often serve it as a dinner party starter with some finely sliced artisan salami and chopped cornichons.

Ingredients
2 tablespoons of mayonnaise – home made or good quality bought mayo.
1 tablespoon of natural yoghurt
1 small head of celeriac, peeled and finely grated in a food processor.
Juice of a lemon
1 tablespoon of Dijon mustard
Handful of chopped flat leaf parsley, lovage or chives
Sea salt and black pepper to taste

Place all the ingredients in bowl, mix thoroughly and season to taste. Set aside in the fridge for an hour or so to allow the flavours to develop before serving.

Summer Coleslaw

I really don't like the type of coleslaw that you get in supermarket delis – taste this and you'll always make your own!
Serves 8

Ingredients
1 small head of white cabbage, finely sliced by hand or in a processor
2 large carrots, peeled and grated
2 banana shallots, finely sliced
Options: add a finely sliced head of fennel or half a small head of celeriac

Dressing
2 tablespoons of mayonnaise
Juice of half a lemon
3 tablespoons of thick Greek yoghurt
Salt and pepper

Mix the sliced and grated salad ingredients together. Mix the dressing and coat the salad thoroughly. Season to taste.

Winter Coleslaw

This is a really unusual and colourful salad and a complete crowd pleaser at a buffet lunch, supper or a BBQ at any time of the year. The dressing is

gorgeous. It is the dish I am most often requested to bring along to potluck gatherings.
Serves 8

Ingredients
A head of celery – washed, de-strung and finely chopped including some of the leaf
1 small red cabbage, finely shredded on a mandolin or in a food processor
1-2 bunches of spring onions, finely chopped including the greens

Dressing
2 tablespoons mayonnaise
3 tablespoons of thick Greek yoghurt
1-2 teaspoons of mild French mustard
Sea salt and black pepper

Mix the chopped salad ingredients together. Mix the dressing and coat the salad thoroughly. Season to taste.

Tomato Salads
I love bright red, juicy tomatoes, especially home grown ones. Just remember - never keep them in the fridge as it destroys the flavour completely, and use a sharp knife to cut them.

Dressing for all the tomato salads
3 tablespoons of red wine vinegar
6 tablespoons extra virgin olive oil
½ teaspoon soft brown sugar
1 clove crushed garlic
Sea salt and black pepper

Summer Tomato
You can't beat this classic combination of ripe juicy tomatoes and basil - summer in a bowl.
500 to 750g ripe tomatoes – thinly sliced
Good handful of fresh basil leaves – torn
Dressing as above.

Layer the tomatoes and basil in a salad dish – spoon over the dressing and allow the flavours to mingle.

Savoury Tomato
This is fantastic with steak and makes a nice change from a classic basil salad, especially in the winter when sage is easier to get hold of.

Serves 4 to 6
500 to 750 g ripe tomatoes – thinly sliced
A good handful of soft, fresh sage leaves – finely chopped
Variation: omit the sage and add 1 finely chopped shallot instead.

Mix the dressing and add to the finely sliced tomatoes and sage. Serve at room temperature.

Tricolore
This salad is the Italian flag on a plate. Until I had this in Italy, I had no idea why it was so popular. I now only make it at home with the best tomatoes and buffalo mozzarella I can buy – delicious!

Serve as a large sharing plate or individual plates as a dinner party starter.
Per person - 1 tomato per person – thinly sliced, 1/2 ball of buffalo mozzarella – thinly sliced, 4 large basil leaves.

Layer a slice of tomato, then a slice of mozzarella interleaved with basil leaves to make it look appetising and attractive. Dress with olive oil and season with sea salt and ground black pepper.

Greek Salad
Served with a bowl of hummus, warm pitta bread and tzatziki, this is a quick summer lunch favourite.

Serves 4

Ingredients
4 ripe tomatoes, halved and quartered
1 small red onion, finely sliced, seasoned and steeped in a tablespoon of red wine vinegar,

a teaspoon of dried oregano and a dash of olive oil to about an hour beforehand to reduce the strong raw onion taste
Half a cucumber, deseeded and cut into quarters lengthwise and then into 1cm thick chunks
175g green olives
200g feta (barrel aged preferably), crumbled
Juice of half a lemon
2 tablespoons of good quality (preferably Greek) olive oil

Arrange the salad ingredients in a serving bowl, dress thoroughly with the oil and lemon juice and seasoning. Crumble the feta over the salad and serve. It won't last long.

Tzatziki/Cacik/Raita

In Greece this yoghurt and cucumber dish is called tzatziki, the Turkish version is called cacik and in India it's called a raita. I use it to accompany any Mediterranean and Middle Eastern dishes or as part of a mezze, or for an Indian menu – it's great as an accompaniment to roast lamb and curries.

Ingredients
½ cucumber, peeled, deseeded and either chopped into small pieces (as a salad dish) or grated (as a sauce/side dish)
Sea salt to season
1 clove of garlic either cut in half and rubbed on the inside surface of the serving dish and used to lightly fragrance the yoghurt or crushed into a paste and mixed in with it for a more garlicky flavour
A handful of fresh mint leaves, very finely chopped
250ml thick Greek yoghurt
Olive oil to dress the Mediterranean version
A drop of cider vinegar
Optional: a sprinkling of finely ground roasted cumin seed or cayenne pepper for the Asian version.

Add the cucumber, mint, garlic, vinegar and yogurt to a dish, mix thoroughly and season to taste. Drizzle with olive oil.

French Red Rice Salad

Nutty and colourful, vegetarians love this dish as a meal by itself and it's also delicious with BBQ meat, sausages and cold cuts.

Serves 4
Equipment: frying pan with a tight lid, bowl for the dressing and a large serving bowl, mortar and pestle
Takes: 60 minutes

Ingredients
275ml Camargue red rice
200g feta cheese
6 spring onions, trimmed and finely chopped – including the greens
Salt and pepper
Dressing
1 clove of garlic, crushed
½ teaspoon of Maldon salt
1 dessertspoon of whole grain mustard
1 tablespoon of balsamic vinegar
2 tablespoons of extra virgin olive oil
Freshly ground black pepper

Cook the rice in the frying pan with 570ml of boiling salted water. Bring it back to a simmer, put the lid on and cook on a gentle heat for 40 minutes.
Turn off the heat and leave to cook in the steam for another 15 minutes.
Make the dressing by crushing the garlic to a paste with the salt. Once it has become a paste, add the mustard, then the vinegar and the seasoning. Finally, mix in the olive oil.
Once the rice has cooked and cooled, pour the dressing over (don't do this while the rice is hot or it will just dilute the flavour completely) and put it in the serving dish.
Sprinkle the finely chopped spring onions and crumbled feta all over the top and serve.

Cucumber, Olive & Walnut Salad
This is a lovely buffet or BBQ salad at any time of the year. It's especially good with cold roast chicken.

Ingredients

1 whole cucumber, peeled, cored and cubed
125 stoned and chopped green olives
75g chopped and shelled Serr walnuts
Optional: 1 ripe avocado, peeled and cubed
Juice of half a lemon
Little gem lettuce – washed and dried
Dressing
170ml of sour cream
3 tablespoons of single cream
2 teaspoons of fresh tarragon, chopped
Olive oil to drizzle
Salt and pepper

Arrange the lettuce leaves on a broad serving plate. Mix the cucumber, lemon juice, olives and walnuts together, spoon over the lettuce. Mix the dressing ingredients together, spoon over the salad. Sprinkle over the tarragon and drizzle with a little olive oil.

Carrot Salad

There are any number of ways of making a big bowl of grated carrots turn into a brilliant summer salad simply by adjusting the combination of oil and vinegar or lemon juice based dressings' or by adding in a few salted peanuts or seeds such as poppy and sesame. This is my favourite version.

Grate about 350g of peeled carrots and season them with a little salt. Heat 2 tablespoons of groundnut or rapeseed oil in a small pan. When it's hot, add in a tablespoon of brown mustard seeds and wait for them to pop (this will only take seconds), pour the seeds and oil over the carrots. Add 2 tablespoons of lemon juice and mix well. Leave it to infuse for about half an hour before serving.

Bean Salad with Lemon & Mustard Dressing

This is a great cold table salad standby at any time of the year. It's best with home cooked beans but tinned still work well if you're in a hurry.

Ingredients

Either 250 g of dried borlotti and haricot beans, pre-soaked overnight, rinse, boil rapidly for 10 minutes then gently boil until tender for about an hour an a half with a bay leaf or

use 2 tins of good quality tinned beans, rinsed
1 large red onion – sliced thinly
325 g French beans cut into 2cm long pieces
Optional – 1 red pepper, sliced in long strips

Dressing
Juice of a lemon
4-5 tablespoons of extra virgin olive oil
1 teaspoon of honey
2 teaspoons of French mustard
Sea salt and black pepper

Cook the dried beans or rinse the tinned ones. Boil the French beans in salted water for 3 minutes and then rinse in cold water, drain. Place the 3 types of beans and onion (plus the pepper if using) in a serving bowl. Mix the dressing ingredients together, coat the salad thoroughly and season to taste.

White Bean & Tuna Summer Salad

I remember eating this for lunch by the pool at a gorgeous hotel in the Italian mountains and charmed the chef into sharing the recipe. The celery leaves, so often overlooked as an ingredient, transform the look and flavour of it. Delicious!

Serves 4
Equipment: mixing bowl
Takes: 20 minutes

Ingredients
1 400g tin of white cannellini beans, rinsed and drained (cooked from scratch is best but tinned are fine!)
2 x 190g tins of good quality tuna, drained
2 celery stalks, finely chopped
A handful of cooked and blanched green beans chopped into 2cm lengths
Leaves from the celery tops, finely chopped
Juice of a lemon
Handful of flat leaf parsley
Sea salt and freshly ground black pepper
3 tablespoons of extra virgin olive oil

Place the beans, green beans, salt, pepper, celery, celery leaf, parsley, lemon juice and 2 tablespoons of the olive oil in a mixing bowl and mix thoroughly.

Spoon into individual serving bowls or on a serving platter, place the tuna on top, drizzle with the remaining oil and a little more ground black pepper.

Potato Salad

Everyone loves a freshly made potato salad, so much nicer than any shop bought version.

This is best made with baby new or Charlotte potatoes. Cook them with a sprig of fresh mint and then drain and cool. Cut the potatoes into small bite-sized pieces. Mix in 4 finely sliced spring onions or chopped chives. Dress with mayonnaise or mayonnaise mixed with a little crème fraîche. Season to taste. Put it in the fridge until you need it or the mayo will turn warm and unpleasant.

A tablespoonful of whole grain mustard mixed in with the mayo makes a delicious change and looks really attractive.

Grandma Foster's Rice & Prawn Salad

Inspired by a recipe served long ago at the sadly now defunct Fishes restaurant in Burnham Market, this has been served up as the centrepiece at dozens of family gatherings and buffet lunches over the years, including Nina's Christening. It's still a favourite. Using good quality prawns and paying attention to the layered presentation is what makes the impact. This needs to be eaten on the day that it is made.

Serves 8

Equipment: a large oval serving platter, 2 mixing bowls - one for the rice, one for the dressing, saucepan for the rice.

Takes: 60 minutes

Ingredients

500g white long grain rice, cooked in salted water (1 teaspoon to the boiling liquid), drain and allowed to cool

350g good quality frozen cooked prawns – defrosted and patted dry on kitchen towel
2 ripe pears – peeled, cored and cut lengthwise into 4 giving you 8 pieces
2 English dessert apples, peeled, cored and chopped into small pieces
Juice of a lemon
½ cucumber – de-seeded and chopped into small pieces
Cayenne pepper

Cream dressing
300ml whipping cream
1 tablespoon of Heinz salad cream (don't be tempted to substitute with mayo, it isn't sharp enough)
2 tablespoons of Heinz tomato ketchup

Cook the rice and when it's cool transfer it to a large mixing bowl.

Make the Marie Rose sauce by whipping the cream and then mixing in the salad cream and tomato ketchup. Adjust to taste - it should be creamy but with the acidity of the salad cream and tomato sauce adding a sharpness. It should be a delicate pale pink colour and just taste of tomato, not be overpowered by it.

Peel and chop the apple and toss it in half the lemon juice to stop it from browning. Add to the rice.

Chop the cucumber into roughly the same size pieces as the apple and add to the rice. Mix this together thoroughly and then spread this out as your base layer onto the oval serving platter.

Peel and quarter the pears and toss these pieces in the rest of the lemon juice to prevent them from going brown too. Arrange the 8 pieces of pear elegantly on top of the rice around the dish so that the narrow ends point into the centre.

Spoon the Marie Rose sauce carefully over the top of the rice and pears so that it covers the top but you can still see the rice mixture underneath – the pears sticking out act as a marker for serving it. Use a palette knife to smooth the top out if necessary.

Now, arrange the prawns on top of the Marie Rose sauce and sprinkle with a scant amount of cayenne pepper.

Refrigerate until you need it.

CHAPTER TEN CAKES & PUDDINGS

"Anything is good if it's made of chocolate."
Jo Brand
(British comedian, writer and broadcaster)

Classic Sponge Cake

It's hard to beat a classic sponge cake for an afternoon tea, a birthday party or a bake sale. This is my favourite recipe. Use good quality butter and eggs to achieve the best flavour.

Equipment: two 19cm sponge tins (approx. 4cm deep), a large roomy mixing bowl. You can use a wooden spoon or an electric hand whisk or a bowl mixer like a Kitchen Aid.
Takes: 20 minutes prep, 30 minutes to cook plus cooling time

Ingredients
110g soft unsalted butter
110g golden caster sugar
2 large eggs, beaten
110g self-raising flour – sift it if you like but modern flour really doesn't need it
1 teaspoon of real vanilla extract
Icing sugar to dust/finish
To fill: My favourite is Bonne Maman blackcurrant conserve and freshly whipped cream, you could use other conserves such as strawberry or raspberry and/or with a few of their fresh fruits added in. Lemon curd and mascarpone cheese also make lovely combinations.

Pre-heat the oven to 170°C
Lightly grease and line the cake tins with baking parchment.
Cream the butter and sugar together until pale and fluffy.
Add a spoon of flour to the mix and then gradually add the beaten egg, add another spoon of flour if it looks like splitting.
Fold in the remaining flour to the bowl – you should now have a soft dropping consistency. If it isn't right add a tablespoon of hot water.
Divide the mixture between the two tins as evenly as you can.
Place them in the oven and they should be cooked in about 25 to 30 minutes. They will feel springy to the touch if you touch them lightly with

your finger.
Leave them to cool on a rack before turning them out and peeling off the baking parchment.
Sandwich them together with the filling of your choice.
Dust with icing sugar before serving.

Classic Chocolate Cake

Make it exactly like the recipe above but leave out the vanilla and replace it with a generous tablespoon of good quality cocoa power like Green & Black's. Sandwich with Nutella melted with a little double cream, or Morello cherry jam and fresh cream.

Chocolate Conserve Cakes

This is one of my favourite chocolate cake recipes and makes either a very good whole cake, or a cupcake style base. I made a giant one for Nina's 18th birthday party which took four hours to cook! Essentially, this is a cake mix flavoured with a jar of your favourite conserve – Morello cherry, orange marmalade, or stem ginger preserve and a bar of dark chocolate. The cake is good enough to go unadorned, but sifted with some cocoa powder, or a slick of melted chocolate and double cream with your favourite chopped nuts or perhaps chopped stem ginger, it looks amazing.

Serves 6 to 8
Equipment: large saucepan, 20cm loose bottomed cake tin lightly greased with the base lined with baking parchment
Takes: 20 minutes prep, 50 minutes baking plus cooling time

Ingredients
125g unsalted butter
150g golden caster sugar
150g self-raising flour
2 large eggs, beaten
100g bar of dark 70% chocolate broken into pieces
Pinch of Maldon salt
Flavouring: 300g Bitter Orange marmalade – Bonne Maman thin cut for preference OR 300g Bonne Maman Black Cherry conserve OR 300g Stem Ginger Preserve

Pre-heat the oven to 180°C.
Carefully melt the butter over a medium heat in a large saucepan.
Add the chocolate pieces and, once it starts to melt into the butter, remove the pan from the heat.
Stir the jam, sugar and salt into the melted butter and chocolate mixture.
Next, stir in the beaten egg and then the flour little by little until it's all combined properly.
Pour into the cake tin and bake on a metal tray in the oven for about 50 minutes, or until a skewer comes out clean (I use a piece of dried spaghetti). Place it on a rack to cool before turning it out.
Decorate with sifted cocoa powder, chocolate cream etc.

Soured Cream & Fruit Conserve Crumble Cake

This is a really good tray bake for parties, school or charity events – it always raises a lot of cash and smiles!

Makes 16 squares
Serve warm or cold
Equipment: 22.5cm x 30cm rectangular cake or roasting tin lined with baking parchment lined and the sides lightly buttered.
2 large mixing bowls
Time: 20 minutes prep, cooks in around 45-50 minutes depending on your oven at 180°C.

Ingredients
Crumble
110g plain flour
40g porridge oats
60g light muscovado sugar
60g caster sugar
Good pinch of sea salt
80 unsalted butter, melted
Cake
280g self-raising flour
1 teaspoon of baking powder
1/2 teaspoon sea salt
284ml carton soured cream
1 teaspoon of vanilla bean extract
60g unsalted butter, melted
180g golden caster sugar

3 large eggs
150g conserve – blackcurrant, apricot, raspberry or cherry all work well

Pre-heat the oven to 180°C.
Grease and line the cake tin.
Make the crumble first by mixing all the ingredients thoroughly in a bowl. Chill this mixture while you make the cake.
Make the cake next – put all the ingredients except the conserve in a large bowl and mix together well until smooth
Spoon into the prepared tin and smooth it down.
Beat the conserve a little to soften it and spoon dollops evenly across the top of the cake mix.
Using a fork lightly feather the conserve across the mixture, taking it right into the edges.
Now spread the crumble mixture over the conserve and cake mix.
Bake in the oven for 45-50 minutes until a skewer comes out clean.
If it looks like it is browning too much, put a little foil loosely over the top.
Cool it in the tin for at least 10 minutes before turning it out.
Cut into 16 squares.
Serve warm or cold.

Banana Cake

It's essential to use very ripe bananas for this recipe to get the full flavour; the browner and spottier the skins the better. I used to make it just to use leftover fruit so that it wouldn't go to waste, then I found out that everyone was deliberately not eating the fruit so that I would have to make it. Crafty little monkeys! You don't have to soak the sultanas in Kahlua, but it really is the secret to the flavour of the cake. The alcohol burns off with cooking so you can give it to children. I keep a bottle in just to make this cake.

Equipment: large mixing bowl, one 23 x 13 x 7cm loaf tin, lightly buttered and the base lined with baking parchment.
Takes: 45 minutes to soak the sultanas, 25 minutes prep, an hour to an hour and a quarter to bake plus cooling time

Ingredients
100g sultanas soaked in 60ml of Kahlua – lightly warm it first so the fruit will absorb

the liquid – takes about 45 minutes
175g plain flour
2 teaspoons of baking powder
½ teaspoon of bicarbonate of soda
½ teaspoon of Maldon salt
125 soft unsalted butter
150g soft brown sugar
2 large eggs, beaten
4 very ripe bananas, mashed
1 teaspoon of vanilla extract

Pre-heat the oven to 170°C.
Mix the flour, baking powder, bicarb and salt together.
Beat the butter and sugar together until fluffy.
Add a tablespoon of the flour.
Gradually stir in the beaten egg and then the mashed banana.
Add the vanilla and the Kahlua soaked sultanas.
Add the flour in batches until completely incorporated.
Pour evenly into the loaf tin and bake in the oven for an hour to an hour and a quarter or until a skewer comes out clean (I use a piece of dried spaghetti).
Place it on a rack to cool before turning it out. Peel off the baking parchment from the base.

Madeira Cake

This is the very best plain buttery cake to my mind. In the (very) unlikely event that there is ever any left over, it makes the most fantastic base for a trifle.

Equipment: mixing bowl and a 23 x 13 x 7cm loaf tin, buttered and the base lined with baking parchment.
Takes: 20 minutes prep, an hour to bake plus cooling time

Ingredients
240g softened unsalted butter
200g caster sugar, plus extra for sprinkling
Grated zest and juice of 1 lemon
3 large eggs, beaten
210 self-raising flour
90g plain flour

Pre-heat the oven to 170°C.
Cream the butter and sugar together.
Add the lemon zest and a spoonful of flour.
Gradually add in the beaten egg with a couple more spoons of flour to stop it from splitting.
Add the remaining flour and then the lemon juice.
Pour it evenly into the loaf tin.
Sprinkle the top with two tablespoons of caster sugar. This gives it a lovely shiny crust.
Bake for an hour in the oven on a metal baking tray for about an hour until a skewer comes out clean.
Cool it on a wire rack before turning it out and remove the baking parchment.

Lemon & Poppy Seed Cake

This is just as lovely is the Madeira cake, made exactly as it is in the recipe above, but with the juice of another small lemon and 2 tablespoons of poppy seeds. Scrummy!

Very Sticky Ginger Cake

This is one of the recipes that originally inspired this book because I only had it scribbled on a scrap of paper that was stained with butter spots and the imprint of an old treacle tin. It is one of my Mum and Dad's favourites and I usually bake one to take when I go up to Lincolnshire to visit them. You can serve it as a pudding with cream or ice cream, or as a cake for afternoon tea.

Cook in the oven at 160°C
Equipment: 20cm x 27cm shallow baking tin (about 5cm) , large mixing bowl, baking parchment
Time: 15 minutes prep, cooks in around an hour depending on your oven

Ingredients
115g unsalted butter
225g plain flour
115g caster sugar

2 large eggs, beaten
227g warmed black treacle (this is equal to half a tin of Lyles treacle- stand the tin in a small bowl of warm water and it will be easier to pour the right quantity out of the tin)
55g finely chopped sultanas
85g finely chopped preserved ginger and 1 dessertspoon of the ginger syrup it comes in (I have been known to use half a leftover jar of ginger preserve with equally good results)
2 teaspoons of ground ginger
2 tablespoon of double cream
½ teaspoon of bicarbonate of soda

Pre-heat the oven to 160°C
Grease the baking tin with butter and line the bottom with baking parchment
Measure out all the ingredients ready for mixing
Finely chop the sultanas and the preserved ginger
Cream the butter and sugar together in a large mixing bowl.
Mix in the beaten egg, warmed treacle, chopped sultanas, preserved ginger and ginger syrup
Sift in the flour and the ground ginger
Turn into the lined baking tin
Place in the oven and leave for approximately one hour or until cooked through. Don't be tempted to open the oven for at least an hour. Test by piercing it carefully with a piece of spaghetti or a fine skewer – if it comes out clean it's cooked.
Once cooked, remove from the oven and leave to cool, preferably on a on a rack, and then turn the cake out of the tin. Store in a cake tin or wrap in foil. It tastes wonderful now but will become more fragrant, delicious and sticky if you leave it for a day or so.

Keiller's Dundee Cake

This is quite the nicest and moistest fruitcake - the only one that Pigeon Cottagers will actually eat! A traditional Dundee cake is actually studded with almonds - we don't like it that way but you can add them if you want to.

Equipment: 20cm cake tin, greased and lined with baking parchment, large mixing bowl.
Cook in the oven at 170°C
Takes: 20 minutes prep, 2 to 2 1/2 hours to cook

Ingredients

150g soft unsalted butter
150g caster sugar
3 large eggs, beaten
225g plain flour
1 teaspoon of baking powder
325 mixed dried fruit – currants and sultanas soaked in a cup of strong hot Earl Grey tea (and a tot of whisky if you like). I leave it overnight and stir occasionally to absorb all the liquid.
50g finely chopped, mixed candied peel
2 tablespoons of ground almonds
Finely grated rinds of an orange and a lemon
Optional: 50 g whole blanched almonds or flaked almonds

Cream the butter and sugar together until light and fluffy.
Add in the eggs a little at a time - add a spoon of flour with each egg to stop it splitting.
Carefully fold in the remaining flour and the baking powder.
Add the soaked, dried fruit, mixed peel, orange and lemon rind and the ground almonds.
If it isn't a good dropping consistency, add a little milk.
Pour it into the cake tin and smooth it out evenly (stud the top with the almonds if you're using them or scatter with flaked almonds).
Place the cake in the centre of the oven on a baking sheet and bake for 2-21/2 hours. The top should be golden and springy. A piece of dry spaghetti or a skewer should come out cleanly if you're in doubt.
Let the cake cool properly before taking it out of the tin.
Once cool, store it in an airtight tin. Keeps well for several days.

English Rice Pudding

This is a proper nursery pudding, the kind that makes you feel warm and utterly comforted just by the fragrance that fills your kitchen when it's cooking. Eating it? Well, that's love in a bowl.

Serves 6
Cook in the oven at 150°C
Equipment: Large oval or square ovenproof dish and a milk saucepan
Takes: 10 minutes prep, cooks in around an hour and a half depending on your oven

Ingredients
100g pudding rice
750ml full cream milk (preferably Jersey)
40g caster sugar (preferably vanilla sugar)
A grating of nutmeg
The seeds from a vanilla pod
20g unsalted butter

Preheat the oven to 150°C.
Lightly butter the baking dish.
Add the rice.
Bring the milk and sugar to the boil.
Pour over the rice, stir in the vanilla seeds.
Grate a light dusting of nutmeg over the top and dot with pieces of butter.
Place in the middle of the oven and bake, uncovered, for about an hour and half until the rice is soft and creamy and the top or 'skin' is golden.

Indian Rice Pudding

Using coconut milk mixed with cow's milk, I serve this just warm or chilled with some ripe mango slices as the dessert course for a curry night dinner party

Serves 6
Equipment: Large oval or square ovenproof dish and a milk saucepan.
Takes: 10 minutes prep, cooks in around an hour and a half depending on your oven

Ingredients
100g pudding rice
350ml full cream milk (preferably Jersey)
1 x 400ml tin of coconut milk
40g caster sugar
A bruised stem of lemon grass
Fruit to serve – sliced fresh mango, banana or strawberries

Preheat the oven to 150°C.
Lightly butter the baking dish.
Add the rice.
Bring the milk, lemon grass and sugar to the boil.
Pour over the rice.

Place in the middle of the oven and bake, uncovered for about an hour and half until the rice is soft and creamy and the top is lightly golden.
Serve just warm or chilled with fruit – sliced mango, banana or strawberries.

Panna Cotta

I have tried many recipes for panna cotta but this one is the daddy of them all. Delicately set with just the right amount of gelatine, it is one of my most requested desserts.

Serves 6
Equipment: to make a traditional turned out panna cotta you will need 6 dariole moulds. Once, when I had loaned mine to someone, I used pretty glass serving dishes instead.
Takes: 45 minutes plus 4-5 hours chilling

Ingredients
1 litre of double cream
4 leaves of gelatine
1 large vanilla pods
150g caster sugar
120ml milk
Zest of 2 oranges
80ml vodka
Fruit coulis (gently cooked and reduced whole fruit with a little sugar that has been passed through a fine sieve to remove the pips and skin) and fresh fruit to serve – raspberries, blueberries, strawberries and blackcurrants are especially good

Soak the gelatine leaves in the milk in a small bowl.
Place 800ml of the cream in a non-stick pan; add the seeds from the vanilla pod, the pod, orange zest and the sugar. Simmer until it has reduced by a third.
Take the gelatine out of the milk. Warm the milk on the hob and then add the gelatine back to dissolve it.
Add the dissolved gelatine to the cream and pass through a sieve to remove the orange zest and vanilla pod.
Lightly whip the remaining cream and fold into the other half along with the vodka.
Pour it into the moulds. If you very, very lightly oil them with a flavourless oil they will come out more easily later.
Leave it to set in the fridge for at least a couple of hours.

Make the fruit coulis and prep the whole fruit.
Take the panna cotta out of the fridge. To un-mould them I usually just dip them very briefly into a bowl of hot water if they don't come out easily by just inverting them on a serving plate.
Serve with the fruit.

Crumble

What could be more a more satisfying English pudding than a classic fruit crumble? When it's cold outside, you'll feel warm inside just at the thought of this dessert.

Serves 4 to 6
Equipment: a 1.75 litre pie or gratin dish
Takes: 20 minutes prep, 30 to 40 minutes to cook.

Ingredients
225g dry ingredients – depending on your tastes mix up plain or wholewheat flour, jumbo oats and/or a tablespoon of ground almonds
75g unsalted butter cut into cubes
85g soft brown sugar (you can add more if you have a sweet tooth but this should suffice)
A little cinnamon added to the topping goes well with apple or plum crumble
Fruit filling and caster sugar – rhubarb and orange, apple and sultana, blackcurrants, blackberry and apple, stoned and halved apricots or plums, gooseberries (sprinkled with a little sugar or elderflower cordial)– whatever is in season or takes your fancy.

Preheat the oven to 180°C
Mix the dry ingredients, sugar and butter together until they resemble fine crumbs – I prefer to do this by hand.
Lightly pre-cook the fruit filling if you're using apples or rhubarb with a little sugar so that it keeps its shape. Blackcurrants, plums or gooseberries can just be placed in the dish with a light sprinkling of caster sugar.
Butter the pie dish and fill with the fruit, then sprinkle on the crumble topping. Use a fork to lightly even it out, don't compress it.
Bake for 30 to 40 minutes until it's toasted and golden brown.
Serve hot with custard.

Fruit Pies

Any of these fillings are also delicious with a sweet short or flaky pastry topping instead of crumble. Readymade pastry is perfectly OK especially if you're really busy, or just not a keen pastry cook like me!

Sponge Puddings

The aroma of freshly baked sponge puddings and custard, mmmm can't beat it! Our favourite has an almond sponge topping but, if you can't eat nuts, the flour based one will be just the job.

Prepare an 850ml pudding dish and add the prepared fruit filling of your choice as in the previous recipes.
Top with either the almond or the flour based sponge mixture. Bake at 180°C for an hour.

Almond Sponge Topping
This one is nicest with apples, apricots or plums.

Ingredients
110g soft unsalted butter
110g golden caster sugar
2 large eggs, beaten
110g ground almonds

Cream the butter and sugar together in a mixing bowl, add a tablespoon of the almonds and then gradually mix in the beaten egg. Gently fold in the rest of the ground almonds.

Vanilla Sponge Topping
This one is good with more or less any fruit base.

Ingredients
110g soft unsalted butter
110g self-raising flour
1 teaspoon of baking powder
110g golden caster sugar
2 large eggs
To flavour: either a teaspoon of vanilla bean extract or the grated zest of an orange (good with a rhubarb base) or lemon zest (good with apple).

Cream the butter and sugar together in a mixing bowl, add a tablespoon of the flour and then gradually mix in the beaten egg. Gently fold in the rest of the flour and the baking powder.

Tubby Custard Sauce

You can't eat an apple pie or a crumble without a good helping of hot vanilla tubby custard. A non-stick milk saucepan is essential for this unless you really like scrubbing pans clean. You can make it with egg yolks, milk and sugar, but this is the everyday cheat's way!

Put 35g of Bird's custard powder and 20g of sugar in a basin. Mix to a smooth paste with a little cold milk. Heat 280ml of milk and the seeds from half a fresh vanilla pod together and then pour that on to the custard paste. It should go thick and smooth. Then add in about 300ml of whipped double cream. Stir and check for sweetness according to your taste.

Banana Tubby Custard

This isn't really a proper recipe, but as children, one of our favourite puddings was a sliced banana in a bowl of this custard. Old traditions pass through the generations, most children still love this.

Chocolate Mousse

This delicious mousse is a classic dinner party, or special family treat favourite. If the serving cups or dishes are pretty then it shouldn't need much, if any, adornment but for a dinner party it looks gorgeous with a little shaved chocolate – milk or white chocolate, some crystallized ginger or chopped pistachio nuts. It can also be served with crisp almond tuile type biscuits or small brandy snaps.

Serves 4
Equipment: Saucepan, 3 mixing bowls and 4 pretty serving dishes – ramekins, tea or espresso cups, glasses etc.
Takes: 30 minutes to make, 2 to 3 hours to set.

Ingredients
4 eggs
220g dark 70% cocoa chocolate (to ring the changes you could make it with the espresso or Maya Gold Green & Black's flavoured chocolate bars)
4 teaspoons of caster or icing sugar (or to taste)
Options: a teaspoon of Tia Maria, Kahlua or dark rum or the juice and grated zest of an orange.

Break the chocolate into small pieces and place over (but not touching) a pan of simmering water. When the chocolate begins to melt, turn off the heat and give it a quick stir to even out any small lumps.
Separate the eggs, being sure not to get any yolk in with the white.
Whisk the egg white into soft peaks and then add in and incorporate the sugar.
Beat the egg yolk lightly and then mix it quickly into the melted chocolate. Add in a third of the egg white to slacken off the chocolate mix and then carefully fold in the rest of the egg white so as to lose any streaks but not the air.
Pour into the serving dishes and leave it to set in the fridge covered in cling film for at least two hours.

Mary's Lemon Mousse Pudding

This recipe came from Grandma Foster's Scottish dancing friend Mary from Aberdeen. It tastes as light as a feather and very lemony. It couldn't be simpler to make, but it does need to be made a few hours ahead of time to allow the lemon mousse and the trifle base to mingle together properly.

Serves: 6 to 8
Equipment: 2 large mixing bowls, pretty glass trifle bowl or individual serving dishes
Takes: 30 minutes prep, chill for 3 hours

Ingredients
397g tin of Carnation condensed milk
3 large eggs
3 lemons
1 pack of Boudoir biscuits, trifle sponge fingers or Ladyfingers

Finely grate the zest from the lemon and then juice them. Strain it carefully to remove any tiny pips or flesh.

Separate the eggs.

Mix the eggs, condensed milk, lemon juice and zest together.

Beat the egg white until stiff.

Gradually fold the egg whites into the egg and lemon mix.

Place a layer of boudoir biscuits in the base of the serving dish and then a layer of the lemon mixture and keep layering until you finish with a final topping of the lemon mixture.

Cover with clingfilm and then put in the fridge for at least 3 hours before you want to serve it.

CHAPTER ELEVEN: FRUIT

"A fruit is a vegetable with looks and money. Plus, if you let fruit rot, it turns into wine, something Brussels sprouts never do".
P.J. O'Rourke
(American satirist, journalist, Managing Editor for National Lampoon)

Most fruits can be eaten either cooked or raw. The more exotic or delicate the fruit, the more likely it is that you'll eat it simply and raw such as mangoes, bananas, pineapple (always best with a dash of lime juice), raspberries, strawberries. Remember never to wash raspberries or you'll turn them into sludge, and never wash a strawberry without the stalk still intact or you'll wash out all the flavour.

Baked Fruit Compotes
Baked fruit is lovely with ice cream or home made natural yoghurt for quick but impressive desserts or breakfasts.

Oven baking fruit means that the pieces will keep their shape and deep flavour. Use as broad and shallow a baking dish as possible and butter it lightly so that the fruit doesn't stick. An hour at about 140°C in the oven will do for most fruits but keep a watchful eye and remove earlier if necessary. About a tablespoon of caster sugar is the most you should need to use to sweeten naturally sour fruits like gooseberries, cooking apples and rhubarb, less for sweeter fruits such as plums and apricots. Adding a touch of alcohol, like rum or Gran Marnier, makes it good enough for a dinner party dessert.

Rhubarb
Wash and cut into 1inch pieces. Layer in the baking dish, cut side down, sprinkle with golden caster sugar, the juice and zest of an orange or a teaspoon of good vanilla essence diluted in a tablespoon of hot water. It is very sour without sugar, but don't overdo it and spoil the delicate flavour. Bake in a low oven c140°for about an hour.

Gooseberries

Wash, dry and layer in the baking dish. Sprinkle with golden caster sugar or a tablespoon of elderflower syrup mixed with another one of water and bake for about 40 minutes at 140°C. Once cooked and cooled, mash the berries with the back of a fork and mix with thickly whipped cream and a tablespoon of custard to make a gooseberry fool.

Plums, Nectarines and Apricots

Wash, dry and halve each plum, nectarine or apricot with a sharp knife and remove the stone. Arrange face up in the bottom of the dish. Sprinkle with golden caster sugar. Bake for about an hour.
Variation: Dot with a few pieces of butter for extra richness of flavour or add a little diluted almond essence or a crumbled amaretto biscuit.

Baked Bananas

Butter the base of a large sheet of baking foil. Peel one ripe banana (the riper the better – it's a great way to use up those ones with spots on the skin that no one wants to eat!) per person and lay them on the foil in the middle. Dot them with butter, a large spoonful of dark brown sugar and scatter over a few sultanas. Adding chopped dates or a tablespoon of dark rum, or my favourite - Kahlua, makes it taste really special. Fold the foil into a parcel so that the ends and the top are sealed. Bake in a hot oven 180°C for about 45 minutes. The butter, sugar and alcohol then turn into a kind of hot toffee sauce. It's delicious served with vanilla ice cream, thick Greek yoghurt or a good dollop of whipped double cream.

Baked Apples

These are lovely at any time of year but brilliant for using up any leftover mincemeat after Christmas.
Serves 4

Ingredients
4 medium sized cooking apples
4 dessertspoons good quality mince meat
20g butter, melted

WHAT'S4TEAMUM?

Preheat the oven to 180°C.
Peel and core 4 cooking apples.
Place them onto a lightly buttered shallow baking dish.
Fill the hollow centres with mincemeat.
Brush the apple with melted butter.
Bake in the oven for about 20 to 25 minutes until slightly soft.
Serve with ice cream or Greek yoghurt.

CHAPTER TWELVE: LEFTOVERS & BUDGET SNACKS

"The most remarkable thing about my mother is that for thirty years she served the family nothing but leftovers. The original meal has never been found".
Calvin Trillin
(American journalist and humourist)

However many people you cook for regularly, there will always be leftovers of some description. There is no need to waste food and these days most people can't afford to either. These are a few of my leftover tips and tricks.

Potato Leftovers
Leftover jackets, new potatoes and mash can be turned into all kinds of tasty treats.

Fish Cakes
Use leftover mash to make store cupboard fish cakes by mixing it with a tin of tuna, some chopped spring onions and capers. Shape into cakes, flour and fry in some oil and butter until crisp on the outside and warm through to the centre.

Bubble and Squeak
Mix mash with leftover green veg like cabbage and sprouts, season and fry in a frying pan with a fat knob of butter with a dash of oil to stop it from burning, serve with a fried or poached egg on top. Yummy.

Croquettes
Mix leftover mash with chopped cold ham, shape them into sausage shapes, coat them in a little beaten egg yolk, and roll them in breadcrumbs. Fry in a little oil and butter.

New Potato Coins
Sliced, cold new potatoes fried in a little oil and butter and sprinkled with

sea salt are delicious with a fried egg and gammon or cold ham or beef.

I also like these sprinkled with cumin and sesame seed and a pinch of cayenne pepper.

Tortilla

Finely slice and slowly and gently fry two large Spanish onions with a large knob of butter and a sprinkling of salt in a medium sized sauté pan with curved sides. Once they are lovely and soft, add in thinly sliced cold potatoes (this can be done with freshly sliced ones on a mandolin too, it just takes longer). While the mixture is still warm, pour over six beaten eggs. Let it mix in, press it down and fry until the bottom develops a golden crust. Once it's cooked, take a flat plate and place it over the pan. Place a tea towel over it and flip it over so the tortilla is now on the plate. Now slide it back in so that the uncooked side can go brown. It's a bit tricky the first time you do it, but practice makes perfect. Once it's cooked, slide it out on to a serving plate. Allow it to cool to room temperature. Serve it cut into wedges. Great with a green salad or a tomato salad.

Variations: add a little wilted fresh spinach or some lightly fried chorizo, garlic and sliced peppers.

Potato Salad

This is best made with baby new or charlotte potatoes. Chop the potatoes into small bite-sized pieces. Mix in 4 finely sliced spring onions or a bunch of chives. Dress with mayonnaise or mayonnaise mixed with a little crème fraîche. Season to taste. A spoonful of whole grain mustard makes a nice change.

Bread leftovers

Having lots of stale bread leftovers isn't a disaster if you know what to do with it.

Breadcrumbs

Blitz the stale bread to fine crumbs in a food processor, mix with grated

Parmesan and use for a gratin topping, add to meatballs or a meatloaf, a sage and onion stuffing, or just freeze them to use another time.

Luxury Cheese on Toast

In a small bowl mix 50ml of cream, 1 tablespoon of beer, 1 teaspoon of English mustard, 225gms of mature grated cheddar, a splash of Worcester sauce and 2 egg yolks. Cut a few thick slices of stale bread; toast the bread on one side under the grill and then top with the cheese mix. Grill until bubbling and golden.

Brushetta

Toast slices of stale Italian or French bread on both sides. Rub with an open slice of garlic and top with chopped ripe tomatoes mixed with olive oil, torn basil leaves and ground black pepper.

Croutons

Cut the crusts off the leftover bread and then into crouton sized cubes. Toss in a little olive oil (or a flavoured garlic or herb oil) and place on a baking tray in a hot oven for about 15 minutes or until crisp and golden. Store in an airtight box and scatter over salads or soup.

Bread Pizza

Cut a few thick slices of stale bread, toast the bread on one side under the grill and then spread with pesto sauce and slices of salami, fresh tomato and mozzarella. Drizzle with olive oil and grill until bubbling and golden.

Fridge & Fruit Bowl Orphans

Open anyone's fridge and you'll probably find quite a few orphan ingredients, or fruit in the bowl that's a bit past its best.

Don't throw away those slightly **wizened vegetables** in the bottom of the crisper, use them for soup, lay a roasting joint on them to make a delicious base for gravy, simmer them with some chicken wings to make a lovely stock for a soup or risotto. Freeze the stock you can't use in those brilliant

'Pour & Store' ziplock freezer bags to use later.

An old rind left over from a chunk of **Parmesan** adds flavour and body when added to a soup.

Leftover cream or crème fraîche can be stirred into mashed potatoes or vegetable purees for extra richness.

Spotty brown **bananas** in the fruit bowl no one wants to eat? Make brilliant smoothies or a banana cake instead.

Peel and cook soft eating apples to make apple sauce to eat with yoghurt or with roast pork. Alternatively, peel and grate them into some 'commuter muesli' for breakfast.

Invest in some decent **freezer quality tubs** and bags so that leftover food you know you definitely won't eat can go in the freezer straightaway, and provides a quick ready meal when you're too busy to cook from scratch.

STORE CUPBOARD TIPS

If you have these basics and favourites in the cupboard, you will always be able to whip up a good simple meal at any time with whatever fresh meat, fish and seasonal vegetables are to hand. It doesn't mean you can't add to them, it's just that these are the most versatile. Even top chefs cheat at home so don't worry about not cooking everything from scratch, or taking a few short cuts.

- Sunflower, rapeseed or groundnut oil for general cooking
- Light olive oil for cooking, extra-virgin for salad dressings
- Unsalted butter for cooking- especially baking
- Wine vinegars for marinades and salad dressings – red, white, cider, sherry and balsamic
- Mustard – English in powder form and French, Dijon and Wholegrain
- Maldon sea salt, white and black pepper
- Fresh garlic
- Tinned tomatoes, cartons of passata, tubes or small tins of tomato puree
- Rice – basmati, risotto, pudding
- Dried pasta – linguine, shells, bows, rigatoni
- Couscous
- Puy lentils
- Eggs, barn or free range preferably
- Stoke's mayonnaise
- Small jar of capers for tuna salads and pasta sauces
- Cheese – Cheddar, feta and Parmesan
- Knorr gel stock pots, Kallo organic chicken and beef stock cubes, Marigold vegetable stock.
- Dried oregano
- Spices – ground cumin, coriander and turmeric, cumin seeds, fennel seeds, fenugreek, dried chilli flakes, smoked Pimentón, chilli powder, cinnamon, caraway, cloves, fresh nutmeg
- Lea and Perrins Worcestershire sauce
- Soy sauce – light and dark
- Thai fish sauce
- Tinned tuna
- Tinned beans – borlotti, black, chickpeas, red kidney, cannellini

- Tinned sweetcorn
- Tinned coconut milk for Thai curries
- Fresh herbs – rosemary, mint, coriander, flat leaf parsley, basil, chives are the most versatile and can be bought in pots and kept happily on a sunny windowsill provided they are watered regularly. There are very good quality frozen versions available now too for perking up a sauce, soup or stew.
- Plain and self-raising flour
- Porridge oats – conservation grade or organic
- Peanut butter
- Golden caster sugar, Demerara and muscovado sugar
- Bonne Maman fruit conserves and the caramel jam all make great ice cream or dessert sauces
- Key staples - bread, cereal, tea, coffee, fruit juice
- Freezer cabinet – frozen petits pois peas, fish, chicken breast, sausages, minced beef, raw prawns, vanilla ice cream.

WHAT'S IN SEASON?

These days, we can buy just about anything all the year round but it doesn't necessarily mean the food will taste all that great. This section shows which food items are best to eat at which time in terms of both flavour and, usually, affordability. Sometimes, the vagaries of the weather throw this off slightly but it is more or less correct. For those items which are obviously not UK grown such as citrus fruits, the month indicates when they are at their best from the imported country of origin.

January & February
- Beetroot, Brussels sprouts, cauliflower, celeriac, celery, chicory, Jerusalem artichoke, kale, leeks, parsnips, potatoes (main crop), rhubarb, swede, turnips.
- Apples, clementines, kiwi fruit, lemons, oranges, passion fruit, pears, pineapple, pomegranate, satsumas, tangerines, walnuts
- Duck, guinea fowl, hare, partridge, venison
- Brill, clams, cockles, haddock, halibut, hake, john dory, lemon sole, monkfish, mussels, oysters, plaice, turbot

March
- Cauliflower, leeks, purple sprouting broccoli, rhubarb, spring onions
- Citrus fruit, Pomegranates, bananas, passion fruit, bananas, kiwi fruit, pineapple
- Cockles, cod, hake, john dory, lemon sole, mussels, oysters, salmon, sea trout

April
- Broccoli, cauliflower, Jersey Royal potatoes, asparagus, radishes, rocket, watercress, sorrel, spinach, spring onions
- Bananas, kiwi fruit
- Cockles, sea trout, cod, john dory,
- Wood pigeon

May

- Asparagus, broccoli, carrots, Jersey Royal new potatoes, new potatoes, radishes, rhubarb, rocket, sorrel, spinach, spring onions, watercress
- Cherries, elderflowers, kiwi fruit
- Lamb, wood pigeon
- Cod, crab, Dover sole, halibut, john dory, lemon sole, plaice, salmon, sea bass, sea trout

June

- Artichoke, aubergine, beetroot, broad beans, broccoli, carrots, courgettes, cucumber, fennel, French beans, garlic, kohlrabi, mange tout, new potatoes, onions, peas, potatoes (main crop), radishes, rocket, runner beans, sorrel, turnips, watercress
- Apricots, blackberries, blueberries, gooseberries, greengages, kiwi fruit, loganberries, melons, peaches, raspberries, redcurrants, strawberries, tomatoes
- Lamb, rabbit, wood pigeon
- Cod, crab, Dover sole, haddock, halibut, herring, john dory, lemon sole, lobster, mackerel, plaice, salmon, sardines, scallops, sea bass, sea trout

July

- Artichoke, aubergine, beetroot, broad beans, broccoli, carrots, courgettes, cucumber, fennel, French beans, garlic, kohlrabi, mange tout, new potatoes, onions, peas, potatoes (main crop), radishes, rocket, runner beans, sorrel, turnips, watercress
- Apricots, blackberries, blueberries, gooseberries, greengages, kiwi fruit, loganberries, melons, peaches, raspberries, redcurrants, strawberries, tomatoes
- Lamb, rabbit, wood pigeon
- Cod, crab, Dover sole, haddock, halibut, herring, john dory, lemon sole, lobster, mackerel, plaice, salmon, sardines, scallops, sea bass, sea trout

August

- Artichoke, aubergine, beetroot, broad beans, broccoli, carrots,

- courgettes, cucumber, fennel, French beans, garlic, kohlrabi, mange tout, onions, peas, peppers, potatoes (main crop), radishes, rocket, runner beans, sorrel, watercress
- Apricots, blackberries, blueberries, greengages, loganberries, melons, nectarines, peaches, plums, raspberries, redcurrants, tomatoes
- Lamb, rabbit, wood pigeon
- Cod, crab, Dover sole, grey mullet, haddock, halibut, herring, john dory, lemon sole, lobster, mackerel, monkfish, plaice, salmon, sardines, scallops, sea bass

September

- Artichoke, aubergine, beetroot, broccoli, butternut squash, carrots, celery, courgettes, cucumber, fennel, garlic, kale, kohlrabi, leeks, mange tout, marrow, onions, peppers, potatoes (main crop), radishes, rocket, runner beans, sweet corn, watercress, wild mushrooms
- Apples, blackberries, damsons, figs, grapes, melons, nectarines, peaches, pears, plums, tomatoes, walnuts
- Duck, grouse, guinea fowl, lamb, rabbit, venison, wood pigeon
- Clams, cod, crab, Dover sole, grey mullet, haddock, halibut, herring, john dory, lemon sole, lobster, mackerel, monkfish, plaice, scallops, sea bass, squid, turbot

October

- Artichoke, beetroot, broccoli, butternut squash, carrots, celeriac, celery, fennel, kale, kohlrabi, leeks, marrow, onions, parsnips, potatoes (main crop), pumpkin, swede, turnips, watercress, wild mushrooms
- Apples, chestnuts, elderberries, figs, grapes, pears, quince, tomatoes, walnuts, sloes
- Duck, goose, grouse, guinea fowl, hare, partridge, rabbit, venison, wood pigeon
- Brill, clams, crab, grey mullet, haddock, halibut, hake, john dory, lemon sole, lobster, mackerel, monkfish, mussels, oysters, plaice, scallops, sea bass, squid, turbot

November

- Artichoke, beetroot, celeriac, celery, chicory, Jerusalem artichoke, kale,

kohlrabi, leeks, parsnips, potatoes (main crop), pumpkin, swede, turnips, wild mushrooms
- Apples, chestnuts, cranberries, elderberries, passion fruit, pears, quince, walnuts
- Duck, goose, grouse, guinea fowl, hare, partridge, pheasant, rabbit, venison, wood pigeon
- Brill, clams, haddock, halibut, hake, john dory, lemon sole, lobster, monkfish, mussels, oysters, plaice, scallops, sea bass, squid, turbot

December
- Beetroot, Brussel sprouts, cauliflower, celeriac, celery, chicory, Jerusalem artichoke, kale, leeks, parsnips, potatoes (main crop), pumpkin, swede, turnips
- Apples, chestnuts, clementines, cranberries, passion fruit, pears, pineapple, pomegranate, satsumas, tangerines, walnuts
- Duck, goose, grouse, guinea fowl, hare, partridge, pheasant, rabbit, venison, wood pigeon
- Brill, clams, haddock, halibut, hake, john dory, lemon sole, monkfish, mussels, oysters, plaice, scallops, sea bass, turbot

WHAT'S4TEAMUM?

KITCHEN EQUIPMENT

"And I find chopsticks frankly distressing. Am I alone in thinking it odd that a people ingenious enough to invent paper, gunpowder, kites and any number of other useful objects, and who have a noble history extending back 3,000 years haven't yet worked out that a pair of knitting needles is no way to capture food?"
Bill Bryson
(Travel writer)

You don't really need very much in the way of equipment to be able to make a halfway decent meal or snack for yourself or a group of friends, and you certainly don't need chopsticks!

It has taken years to build up my own extensive collection of culinary hardware, and the following list includes things I'd find it annoying or simply impractical to manage without these days. You do get what you pay for with kitchen equipment – buy the best quality you can, look after it and it will give you years of faithful service.

- A set of at least three good quality metal saucepans of various sizes with lids. Don't skimp on this purchase – good ones will last for years.
- A couple of ovenproof casserole dishes in different sizes – cast iron ones by e.g. Le Creuset are brilliant for distributing the heat evenly and for 'oven to table' dining
- Non-stick milk pans
- Non-stick frying pans (a large one and an omelette pan)
- A non-stick wok for quick stir-fries
- Non-stick loaf tin – optional to make cakes and meat loaf
- Large metal roasting dish – anodised metal is light, easy to clean and doesn't buckle
- Various sizes of heavy non-stick metal bakeware and baking trays
- Toaster
- Electric kettle
- Can opener
- A waiter's friend type corkscrew
- Vegetable peeler – the type with a 'U' shaped handle and a tilting blade
- Bread knife
- Chopping knifes – Global and Sabatier for preference

- Kitchen scissors
- Chopping boards – dishwasher-proof, plastic
- Silicon spatulas
- Non-stick fish slice
- Wooden spoons in different sizes
- A potato masher (a ricer is also a useful gadget)
- A combination hand-held blender, chopper and whisk
- Metal and non-stick balloon whisks
- A large metal colander
- Dishwasher and microwave proof crockery - plates, mugs, cereal bowls
- Dishwasher proof cutlery – knives, forks, spoons
- Good quality glasses – for smoothies, wine or juice
- Large mixing bowls
- Graters – box grater and a microplane for fine grating
- Pyrex measuring jugs
- Digital weighing scales
- Mortar and pestle
- Metal citrus juicer
- Fine metal mesh sieves
- Click-lock airtight plastic storage boxes
- Splatter guard
- Defrosting tray
- Cling film, foil, baking parchment, Teflon cooking mat, those plastic bags to make ice cubes in

I also have a food processor, a yoghurt maker, an ice cream maker and a pasta maker. They aren't truly essential, especially if you don't have a lot of room in your kitchen, but they are all well worth treating yourself to or putting on your gift wish list.

CONVERSION TABLES

Metric to imperial
30g = 1 oz
110g = 4 oz
450g = 1lb
1 fl.oz = 30ml
5 fl.oz or 1/4pt = 150ml
20 fl.oz or 1pt = 600ml

Oven temperatures
130C = 110C fan = 250F = Gas mark 1
150C = 130C fan = 300F = Gas mark 2
180C = 160C fan = 350F = Gas mark 4
190C = 170C fan = 375F = Gas mark 5
200C = 180C fan = 400F = Gas mark 6
220C = 200C fan = 425F = Gas mark 7
230C = 210C fan = 450F = Gas mark 8

American spoon measures
15g flour = 1 level tablespoon flour
28g flour = 1 heaped tablespoon flour
28g sugar = 1 level tablespoon sugar
15g butter = 1 level tablespoon butter

American liquid measures
240ml = 1 cup US
480ml = 1 pint US
950ml = 1 quart US

American solid measures
125g flour = 1 cup flour
225g butter = 1 cup butter
170g sugar = 1 cup sugar
100g icing sugar = 1 cup icing sugar
170g rice = 1 cup uncooked rice
100g chopped nuts – 1 cup chopped nuts
150g fresh breadcrumbs = 1 cup fresh breadcrumbs
140g sultanas = 1 cup sultanas

ACKNOWLEDGEMENTS

To my family and friends for whom it gives me such pleasure to cook.

To all the cookery writers who have informed and inspired me over the years.

To Kate Welford for designing the artwork for Pigeon Cottage Kitchen.

Lastly, thanks to the hard working farmers and food producers who make it possible for all of us to source high quality ingredients for our tables every day.

ABOUT THE AUTHOR

Nina's Mum (or Janet Davies as she is better known in the adult world) has been churning out delicious snacks and fabulous feasts for friends and family for more than thirty years.

In addition to her other full time job of being an international business superstar, she is also a dab hand with a paintbrush, sews on a mean button and runs a busy 'offspring chauffeuring' service otherwise known as 'Hengrave Cabs'.

Nina's Mum lives at Pigeon Cottage in Suffolk with the 'Stickman' who is (luckily) very good at fixing scratches on cars, chauffeuring, furniture removal, serving drinks and crosswords.

Since this book was first published, as a Kindle edition, Janet now writes a popular cookery blog Pigeon Cottage Kitchen, www.pigeoncottage.com. You can subscribe to the blog, follow her on twitter @pigeoncottage, or on Facebook at pigeoncottagekitchen.

Printed in Great Britain
by Amazon